Prophetic Words *for* KINGDOM *Millionaires*

Dr. JoLynne Whittaker

© 2022 CLARION CALL BOOKS LLC

Book Author:
Dr. Jolynne Whittaker
Book Title:
PROPHETIC WORDS for KINGDOM MILLIONARES
All rights reserved. No part of this publication may be reproduced, stored in a retrieval system or transmited in any form or by any means, electronic, mechanical, photocopying, recording or otherwise without the prior permision of the publisher or in accordance with the provisions of the Copyright, Designs and Patents Act 1988 or under the terms of any licence permitting limited copying issued by the Copyright Licensing Angency.

Published by:
CLARION CALL BOOKS for JoLynne Whittaker Ministries

ISBN-13: 978-0-9991197-4-7

ISBN-10: 0-9991197-4-5

Prophetic Words *for* KINGDOM *Millionaires*

TABLE OF CONTENTS

Introduction..1

Chapter One
The Multi-Faceted Reality of A Wealth Anointing.............................7

Chapter Two
The Millionaire Anointing: Increase and Impact..............................25

Chapter Three
The Uncommon Characteristics of a Kingdom Millionaire..............35

Chapter Four
Discernment and Stewardship: Tools To Multiply Your Money.......51

Chapter Five
You Will Encounter Explosive Increase...61

Chapter Six
Supernatural Secrets That Open Doors...83

Chapter Seven
A Massive Wealth Transfer Is Coming..97

Chapter Eight
The Wealth Anointing Is A Power Position 113

Chapter Nine
The Power of Prophetic Words and Instructions...........................123

Chapter Ten
Your Holiness Is A Weapon..143

Chapter Eleven
God Will Reveal Methods and Strategies
So You Can Access Wealth...157

Chapter Twelve
Urgent Prophetic Words for You… Right Now!............................167

DR. JOLYNNE WHITTAKER

INTRODUCTION

God bless you!

I am so glad you are holding this resource, for the words on these pages are soaked with sound Biblical doctrine and Holy Ghost fire! This is a book for God's high flyers, His eagles in the earth, Royal Kingdom Ambassadors who carry a financial anointing.

Is that you? Are you destined to be a Kingdom Millionaire?

For many of God's people, this is strongly connected to your identity and assignment in the earth, according to *Ephesians 2:8-10*. This may explain some of your childhood experiences and battles you've fought, which we will go into later.

I declare your battles are turning to wins, your trials are turning into triumphs! This is your turning point season, in Jesus' name!

Now before we get started, let me sow these prophetic words into your life. Please read the scriptures and test these words yourself, so you will readily receive them for the glory of God!

The Millionaire Anointing will add so much to your life, but primarily it will allow you to do three things.

1

You will dominate in life. You will not be disempowered or limited. You will not be easily controlled or blocked. The wealth God gives you will empower you as a leader everywhere you go, in every season and every scenario. People will see your status and think twice about messing with you.

Deuteronomy 8:18
But remember the LORD your God, for it is he who gives you the ability to produce wealth… (KJV)

Deuteronomy 28:10
Then all peoples of the earth shall see that you are called by the name of the LORD, and they shall be afraid of you. (NKJV)

2

You will be empowered to fulfill your assignment. You will have what you need at all times, which will allow you to move forward quickly and without hindrance. As you continue to work in the realms God assigns you to, He will prosper the work of your hands and you will abound in every good work and in your destiny.

2 Corinthians 9:8
And God is able to bless you abundantly, so that in all things at all times, having all that you need, you will abound in every good work. (NIV)

3

Your life will demonstrate God is a good God who blesses His people.

Proverb 10:22
The blessing of the Lord brings wealth, without painful toil for it. (NIV)

Hebrews 11:6
But without faith it is impossible to please Him; for he that cometh To God must believe that he is, and that he is a rewarder of them that diligently seek him.

For too long, there has been unnecessary poverty in the Church. It has always been a satanic agenda to disempower and minimize God's people. That satanic assignment is over, in Jesus' name!

I believe this book is for you, and I believe it has come into your hands right on time. *Prophetic Words for Kingdom Millionaires* will be a great tool for you as the Lord increases you and prospers you greatly in this season.

Godspeed and God bless you; may the Lord protect and prosper you most abundantly, and may He use you mightily for His Kingdom purposes. Blessings upon you and your family.

If you're ready to get started, the Lord has so much for you within the pages and chapters of this book. Grab your Bible, buckle up and let's go!

In Jesus' name and in His service,
Dr. JoLynne Whittaker

DR. JOLYNNE WHITTAKER

Chapter One

The Multi-Faceted Reality *of* A Wealth Anointing

DR. JOLYNNE WHITTAKER

In order to function at your full capacity within the blessing, challenge and access of this anointing, you will have to accurately understand what it gives. The wealth anointing does not just give you the money to do God's work in the earth, it outfits and adorns you with other things, too. Learn the fullness of this anointing, in order to flow in the fullness of your identity within it. When you do so, you will be a strong tool in the hand of the Lord and a shining gem for Christ in the earth.

2 Chronicles 20:20
...Hear me, O Judah, and ye inhabitants of Jerusalem; Believe in the Lord your God, so ye shall be established; believe His prophets, so shall ye prosper.

I have noticed a consistent ideology in the body of Christ regarding prosperity and especially regarding the acquisition of wealth (two different financial levels) and that is this: God gives you big money to do big things, and that's the only reason He gives it to you.

To put it more specifically, I have heard people say again and again, "Yes, God will give you big money for your purpose, and to do His work." This is consistently said as if it's fact. What's funny is that people have said it directly to me, as if they are informing me or reinforcing what they assume I already know. This comes from life-long or perhaps years-long programming to believe that Christians are poor, Christians are supposed to be poor, because that's all part of the humble lifestyle of following Jesus.

Undoubtedly that belief was espoused and taught by a pastor who did not walk in the prosperity of the Lord, did not have a revelation of it, and therefore could not impart it to his or her people.

I have noticed people often covertly criticize what they don't know or don't have. Imagine doing so! That person immediately cuts themselves off from learning something new and going somewhere new in their life! I thank God your mind and heart are open to what the Word of God teaches us about life more abundantly. We truly must become like little children so the

Lord can teach us. Hallelujah! *Matthew 18:3*

I'm going to break this down into three categories. These categories accurately and clearly convey the three facets I have discovered to date, regarding the wealth anointing. Let's go.

1 Wealth begins to flow to you as a result of your obedience within the supernatural structure of the Abrahamic Covenant and as a product of your faith.

Abraham, the son of a former idol maker, had given his life to the God of Israel and that brought about a radical transformation in his life. It changed his entire destiny! The Lord singled out (then) Abram just as He has singled out many of you, and established covenant with the man, who saw God's blessing manifest in his life. In Genesis 12, we see the Lord giving Abraham the directive to go to a specific land. By the time we get to Genesis 13, we find that over the natural flow of things within his covenant with the Lord, Abraham has become very rich in cattle, silver, and gold — in other words, God had made Abraham not just rich but very rich, in the hottest commodities of the day. What a setup for impenetrable success! That is what the wealth anointing will do.

With that success came the need for employees and infrastructure. Abraham could do this easily. The wealth anointing sets you up to operate successfully. See that. An operation of any size comes with challenges, responsibilities, presence, excellence, etc. You'll need to be investing back into the operation so that it continues to thrive and do so in excellence. As you grow, you will need more things - space, equipment, staff, etc. The wealth anointing answers those needs. See that.

So, the millionaire anointing allows you to be in the world but not of the world; you're doing business and thriving from Covenant with Jehovah, not the systems of this world. You may sell to the world, you may engage with the world, you will certainly and inevitably impact the world, but you are not reliant upon it. The wealth anointing has set you apart and set you on high. - *Deuteronomy 28:9-14*

So, your wealth and success are simply your IDENTITY as a child of God, as a result of covenant. It has not been given to you only for a specific purpose. It has come to you and multiplied in your life, because God has made the provision for you to access this life of being the head and not the tail, a lender and not a borrower, with all the work of your hands blessed — because that's Who He Is, what He has given you access to, and your obedience has caused it to come forth. If you never do anything else as a wealthy Christian but live holy, live clearly blessed, share Jesus and never deny Him, then that will be enough. Your wealth has come to you because God made the provision for it within covenant.

2 You now have the ability to fulfill your destiny and do whatever God tells you to do. If He tells you to bless someone, you can do it without hesitation. If God tells you to sow generously into a ministry or minister, you can do so cheerfully and easily. If the Lord calls you to build something, fund something, or become the leader in your family who helps lift your bloodline out of impoverished living, you can do so. Your wealth anointing has made you a tool in the hand of Jesus. With this comes great empowerment, and cause for great caution. Read on.

Back in November of 2015, when the Lord began speaking to me about Favor and Prosperity, He illustrated this to me very clearly. I walked into church one Sunday and I heard the Lord tell me to look around. The church was packed. Holy Spirit illuminated something to me: He showed me how some people were very prosperous, and others were struggling financially if not in poverty. I knew the pastor operated in the prosperity anointing, so this was quite puzzling to me, but Holy Ghost helped me understand, immediately. Some receive and some do not; some will work the principles and pursue the Blessing, others will not. It is that simple… that profound… that mind-blowing and that sad.

I sat on the front row, looking around at the people. Again I heard the voice of the Lord tell me to look at one person in particular, an elderly woman. He said, *You are to bless that woman with $200*. Of course I said, *Yes, Lord*. I didn't have it with me so I planned put $200 in an envelope and give it to her at the Wednesday night service. I knew she would be there, because she and her husband and often their son, were always in every service.

Back then, I couldn't just grab $200 and give it to someone. I didn't have it, always. But I had just launched my ministry and our financial flow was growing; I told Jon I needed $200, I told him why, and Jon readily gave me the $200 in cash. As long as I live, I'll never forget what happened next.

Wednesday night came, and we went to church. We took our seats on the front row where we always sat. People flowed into the church and I tried not to keep turning around every 2 seconds to look for the elderly woman. I thought, just let the all the people come, then look for her. I knew she would be there. Worship started and there I was, with that $200 cash burning a hole in my purse! I had to get it to her! I was gripped to do so by the Holy Ghost!

I turned to scan the crowd… and there she was. My eyes locked onto her location and I planned to make a bee-line to her as soon as pastor closed the service. I did so, and the exchange that ensued is forever emblazoned on my heart.

As I approached her, I must have had one intent

look on my face because her eyes widened with fearful expectation. You see, she didn't know me and must have been wondering why I was literally pushing through the crowd to get to her with a desperate look on my face! Looking back, I laugh, but what happened next is no laughing matter.

I stood in front of the woman and extended the sealed envelope to her. I said, "Ma'am, the Lord told me to give this you. God bless you." It was an awkward moment, to be sure. Without any more words, I walked away. I returned to my front seat where Jon was talking to some people and gathering his things. I sat down... then couldn't help but turn around to look at the woman. She was sitting, staring blankly in her seat, her eyes filled with tears.

As I left the church, she stopped me and said, "Thank you. We didn't know how we were going to have our Thanksgiving dinner. We didn't have any money to buy a turkey. We didn't know how we were going to have our dinner this year..." She then told me - in a gush of emotion - that she'd just lost her son in Florida, she'd tried to get to him before he died but he'd passed away without his momma, and now the family was struggling in the aftermath of loss.

An elderly couple. One son passed away. The other son working to try and support his elderly parents. Still, they didn't have enough for a Thanksgiving dinner. No doubt those people of faith were believing the Lord to provide. The Lord used me to do so. I learned a powerful lesson that night and I've never forgotten it:

When God gives seed, He gives it to the Sower. Someone He knows will give. Someone He has already watched and observed to be a cheerful giver. I have never met a prosperous or wealthy Christian who is not also a very generous giver.

I believe you will be that way as well, and this is just another way you will use the wealth God gives you. Be sensitive to the voice of the Holy Ghost. Always give when He tells you to give, and give exactly what He tells you to give. When God speaks to you about a seed, He always has a harvest in mind.

The one who receives will receive the harvest of their prayer or need being answered.

The one who gives, has just sown into a harvest that will come forth in their own future. They may not have done it intentionally and that may have not been their motive or a thought on their mind at all... but that is indeed what will happen, for that is God's system in place.

See this.

Proverb 11:25
A generous person will prosper;
whoever refreshes others will be refreshed. (NIV)

The liberal soul shall be made fat: and he
that watereth shall be watered also himself. (KJV)

Does the size of what you give, matter?
Does the size of what you give have an effect of what returns to you?
Yes, it absolutely does.

When you pour generously as the Lord instructs you to, does that generous pour result in a generous harvest? Yes, of course it does.

Just as with sowing seed intentionally for a harvest, the seed you sow into others as an act of generosity or obedience, will likewise produce a harvest. And the harvest will of course be according to the measure (size) of the of seed planted or given. This is the great seed time and harvest principle, designed to prosper us by the Lord Himself! — *Genesis 8:22*

Giving to others utilizes the same divine reciprocal system; for this reason, generous givers and Sowers, reap a generous, abundant harvest. Selah.

Luke 6:38
Give, and it will be given to you. A good measure, pressed down, shaken together and running over, will be poured into your lap. For with the measure you use, it will be measured to you. (NIV)

Luke 6:38
Give, and it shall be given unto you; good measure, pressed down, and shake tother, and running over, shall men give into your bosom. For with the same measure that ye mete withal it shall be measured to you again. (KJV)

And so, what you give returns to you, multiplied.

I have watched many people give sparingly or "safely", and remain in poverty or lack.

I have seen many of these do so consistently, hoping their level will change. Small seeds produce small harvests, this is a truth many do not want to hear. Inevitably someone will bring up the widow's mite and how that small seed given, was seen as sacrificial to Jesus. Yet unless one is a literal widow giving literally the last of what they have, their small seed does not meet the criteria of the widow's mite.

At some point, each individual has to make the decision to break out of the low-money cycle or level they're in, and take the leap of faith. It is a ledge many don't want to stand on, but in the pursuit of financial prosperity by the hand of the Lord, it is an inevitable destination. God will require a leap of faith from every single person who wishes to receive from Him; this is the means by which a person's fortitude and trust in the Lord, is not merely spoken, but displayed.

I have watched people in poverty or lack sow themselves out of no money, into an abundance of money.

So too have I watched people sow strategically, that is intentionally in terms of the ground and amount of seed they sow, and reap absolutely mind-blowing harvests.

I take note of the many people under my ministry who have learned the accurate Biblical sowing principles I teach, as many of these people are now financially abundant and have begun to be strategic Sowers who live continually in the harvest and overflow of seeds sown perhaps even years ago. Seed has no expiration date; once sown into good soil by a righteous hand, that seed will perform within the Lord's timetable.

Many who carry the Millionaire Anointing have learned to sow strategically and continually, thereby entering into a lifestyle of constant harvest.

As I write these words, I give glory to God; *oh what a strategic God He is!*

3 **The wealth anointing equips you to fulfill your destiny. When it's God's will, it's God's bill. Where God guides... He provides. Many will realize their wealth is a result of their covenant with the Lord, a means by which to be a blessing to others, and they will also realize it is the means by which they will fund their Kingdom Assignment.**

Back in November of 2015, when the Lord began speaking to me about Favor and Prosperity,

As you continue to seek first His Kingdom and righteousness, every resource you need to accomplish, build, execute, launch or access, the things God puts on your heart, will show up right on time. —*Matthew 6:33, Philippians 4:19*

DR. JOLYNNE WHITTAKER

Chapter Two

The Millionaire Anointing: Increase and Impact

DR. JOLYNNE WHITTAKER

You did not get here by accident. Your abundant financial status is a destination you reached by taking specific steps, consistently, on a specific path. The millionaire who has been prospered by the Lord, has achieved that position through obedience, persistence, excellence and pursuit.

Don't ever stop pursuing! Fight, at all costs, to stay hungry. Be grateful, always grateful. But life with God in the mega-money arena, is one of constant increase. Consistently you will see battles won, new dimensions will be accessed, and this will be followed by more increase, as you continually grow, stretch and mature, spiritually.

An earmark of the early Church, was boldness. Another earmark was consistent increase.

As a financially abundant Christian, those two earmarks must always be strong in your life: boldness of faith and in spirit, perpetual increase in the things of God and your resources, as you go from glory to glory in destiny with Christ Jesus.

We know that God rewards those who diligently seek Him. No doubt your current position can be called a very personal and pleasing reward. As you go even higher in your destiny and contributions to the Kingdom of Jesus Christ, the Lord will continue to reward your diligent seek.

This is a prophetic word for you, right now. This is a word for your current season. Your level is changing, your anointing is increasing; God wants to take you somewhere new in the earth for His purposes! I encourage you to get ready - for in the name of Jesus, I declare to you, as you continue to diligently seek the Lord, more rewards are coming! —*Hebrews 11:6*

Your diligent seek has got you here, and your diligent seek will take you further. Let's talk about your growth. For the Lord has impressed upon me, it is expedient that you grow in preparation for new wine! More is coming for your life!

At its' core, I've learned the Millionaire Anointing is for sure 3 things:

1 The Millionaire Anointing is fought by the devil. A faith-filled, Spirit-filled Christian is a whole problem for hell; a faith-filled, Spirit-filled, awake and wealthy Christian, is a downright threat! Many who will read this book can testify that revelation of true, holy, Biblical prosperity, was fought - many voices speak against it but very few accurately divide the Word and teach it.

2 The Millionaire Anointing is intended to be a position of ongoing Godly increase. We'll talk more about this in a later chapter. A mindset of continual growth will be required; with this in place, the Lord will take you into rooms and realms that will blow your mind and bless your heart. God has absolutely no limits; He can take you as high as you are willing to go… as high as you are willing to grow.

3 The Millionaire Anointing is a position of impact. _Poverty_ is a satanic agenda to disempower and destroy people; poverty beats you down and makes you dependent on others, even hopeless to the point of desperation, depression and self-destruction. _Mediocrity_ is a demonic agenda that is intended to disenfranchise and discourage people to the point of complacency or futility. By stark and supernatural contrast, _Kingdom Wealth_ is a position of empowerment for some of God's people, the ones who are called to be impactful in your life and in the areas God instructs you to occupy and act. Kingdom Wealth will never bring overwhelming toil or sorrow, nor should it ever be a source of guilt, because the blessing of the Lord makes men and women rich, and because it's from the Lord, there will be no sorrow with it — it's clean money, it's authorized wealth. And when you have it, you become a person who cannot be intimidated, manipulated or turned away; to the contrary, you are one who anointed and impactful by and with the blessing of God Himself.

I have found that many desire this anointing, but not so many are willing or able to access and occupy it. The Lord quickens me to recall the scripture that says, Many are called, few are chosen. —*Matthew 22:14*

Common Qualities Found in those who carry the Millionaire Anointing:

In the course of my time in ministry, I have met several people who authentically walk in this anointing. All of them have these things in common:

Holiness and Reverence — they love Jesus with a great passion, they love to live holy
A strong command of the Word (they are lovers and students of the Bible)
Righteousness, which brings also Righteous Indignation for what God calls evil
Godly wisdom — they do not rely upon their own understanding but rather, the Word
A Consecrated life — they live completely for the Lord
A natural hunger — they are 100% Kingdom but often business minded as well
Strong honor and integrity — they are people of character and it shows

They are big Sowers, big givers (and always have been)
They are very unique — unlike anyone else and comfortable in being set apart
They are high flyers — no drama, no mess, they are eagles
Their heart is just different — they are both humble and fierce at the same time

These are just some of the qualities I have noticed Kingdom Millionaires have in common. Does any of this sound like you? Are these traits and attributes you embody now, or are you in the process of developing them? I understand now, this position is a calling. Is God calling you to this empowered and impactful financial realm?

Without doubt, some of you will be called to occupy positions of influence and authority in the earth. You will go into industries and spheres of influence.

Some of you will be placed in proximity to people in authority, like Daniel, Joseph or Esther.

You will be positioned for such a time as this, and God will use you greatly.

Some of you will be used to fund the Kingdom Agenda, all the while shifting and redeeming the financial identity and destiny of your bloodline. God will use you to bring Salvation and Blessing by King Jesus, and no longer will generational curses run in the family, but rather Generational Blessings!

I'm glad you picked up this book.
God has something for you within these pages.
Let's go deeper.

DR. JOLYNNE WHITTAKER

Chapter Three

The Uncommon, Unlikely and Characteristic Aspects of a Kingdom Millionaire

DR. JOLYNNE WHITTAKER

God has a sense of humor.
He also likes to make a statement.

Prideful people always think they know what is best, and they think they know *who* is best. The prideful who are wise in their own eyes, often dismiss someone based upon outward appearances or assumptions. We know God looks at the heart when choosing a vessel.

I've also noticed the Lord likes to take someone who is very uncommon and unlikely, and use them to do significant things. God will take an underdog who seems unqualified and undesirable, someone people have rejected, yet God will do prolific things for and through that person.

The Word of God puts it this way:

1 Corinthians 1:27
But God chose the foolish things of the
world to shame the wise;
God chose the weak things of the world
to shame the strong. (NIV)

You may have been rejected by people, perhaps you were made to feel like you're not capable of much.

Some of God's financially anointed, have come from very rocky beginnings, homes that were broken by dysfunction, poverty, sin or abuse.

Some of His chosen vessels, come from a sinful past, full with mistakes and heartache. In that dark place, it was the strong hand of the Lord that lifted you out of the miry clay, saved you from your destructions, and set your foot upon the solid rock of Jesus Christ. Now you're on a new, beautiful, anointed path!

I declare over you today, your place of origin matters not; your renewed identity and rebirth in Christ is all that matters. Your sins are as far removed as the east is from the west. You are a brand new creature in Christ. The Lord remembers your past no more!

Not only that, but your history cannot disqualify you from destiny. God will turn it all around for you and qualify you for your calling!

Like me, you may have been told you were good for nothing and made to feel unwanted and low. Christ Jesus will lift you high, renew your mind, launch you into your destiny, and anoint you to be a millionaire, even a multi-millionaire! Talk about a triumphant return - imagine going back to your old neighborhood, or the town you grew up in, only this time you're going back as a brand new you, with an anointed destiny in the Kingdom of God!

I have met other Kingdom Millionaires, and my ministry has launched Kingdom Millionaires. Two common traits many of us carry, is that we are uncommon and considered unlikely.

We don't fit in, but that's because we're not supposed to.
We never felt completely at home in the world, because we're not.
We are most at home in the presence of God, and we encounter Him in any number of places - from our prayer closet to the church sanctuary, to a beach at sunrise.

Our past instability has made us hungry for the stability that Christ Jesus gives, and our lack of loyalty from others, has made us people who are fiercely loyal to the ones we love and the God we serve.

Another defining characteristic of a Kingdom Millionaire, is our impeccable habits of tithing and giving. We understand the tithe directive and operative principles: we are to bring all the tithe into the storehouse (that means our tithe goes to a minister or a ministry) and we respect the ratio God set: a tenth. We do not attempt to manipulate or avoid the terms, because we understand the tithe is not a suggestion but a directive. We also understand the tithe unlocks and releases two specific blessings that nothing else can.

The first blessing unlocked by the tithe, is the opening of the windows of Heaven. Heaven has an unlimited supply. Heaven has resources that are unimaginable to we on earth. When the windows of Heaven open over a person's life, God pours out a blessing we don't have room enough to contain; we are catapulted into exponential abundance and overflow, to the tune of legacy and estate. —*Malachi 3:10*

The second blessing unlocked by the tithe, is that God rebukes the devourer for our sakes. Monetary attacks do not occur in the way the used to, because they no longer can. Satan has no access point to the blessing released by the tithe, because the Father Himself protects it on our behalf. —*Malachi 3:11*

Not tithing closes off the unlimited Heavens blessing, and it leaves us open and vulnerable to demonic attacks on our finances. None of that is an option for us.

Others may comfortably not tithe, but we cannot do so. Our financial anointing is too strong and too abundant; we must position ourselves for supernatural protection!

Others may say they can't afford to tithe, but we are wise enough to see it accurately: we can't afford *not* to tithe. This incredible supernatural arrangement has been given to us by God as an access point to extreme blessing. We are Kingdom Millionaires; extreme blessing is our comfort zone. Extreme blessing is our lane and we do everything we can to navigate ourselves to that lane, and then we stay there. The tithe never depletes us, to the contrary, it supernaturally adds to us in ways others can't comprehend… and we see financial miracles that elude the masses. Glory to God!

This same obedience and diligence applies to our giving. We are generous givers, abundant Sowers. It is in our nature to give, and we believe just as Jesus said — to us, it is more joyful to give, than to receive. Hallelujah!

Many of us have loved giving gifts and blessing others, ever since we were children. As adults, we revel in being a blessing, and we receive so much joy by sowing into the Kingdom.

We give because it is our design and disposition to do so. However, the giving principle is abundantly at work in our lives, as can be seen by the exponential level of blessing and giving that comes back to us!

For the harvest principle is written and it is sure:

Luke 6:38
Give, and it shall be given unto you; good measure, pressed down, and shaken together, and running over, shall men give unto your bosom. For with the same measure that ye mete withal it shall be measured to you again.

I will never forget the time I sat in a packed church in Tampa, when the spirit of the Lord came upon me. I heard the Lord tell me to take off my shoes and put them on the altar. Moments later, the confirmation came when a leader across the aisle took of his shoes and put them on the altar. Immediately I got up, determined to be obedient. The year was 2018. I was wearing my very first pair of Louis Vuitton shoes. I walked to the altar, slipped off my Louis pumps, placed them upon the altar, then walked bare foot back to my seat.

Our giving started an avalanche of giving. I watched as people came up, placing sport coats and jackets, jewelry and purses, upon the altar. I watched, until my shoes were buried and I could see them no more.

It didn't take long. Several weeks later, I was gifted a shopping trip to a Louis Vuitton boutique in West Palm Beach, Florida. I walked out with not one, not two, but three beautiful new items. The Lord did it! Just last night, I purchased a pair of Louis pumps for myself, to complete my attire for an upcoming preaching engagement. The sales clerk told me over the phone, "I don't know if you have ever owned a pair of Louis Vuitton pumps before, but they do run small…" I replied without thinking, "Oh, I own several pair —" *and I do.*

It all began by putting my first pair on the altar. Where did they go? Who got them?
Who knows? Who cares?!
My experience says it all: since that giving in

2018, I have been reaping a harvest of Louis Vuitton, specifically!

Another time, a staff member contacted me one snowy Saturday night. Their vehicle was in need of repair, and they had two small children. Would I help them pray for the Lord to provide? I knew they were really asking for my help.

That night, I awoke in the wee hours to the familiar leading of the Lord. *Give,* said God. *Give them your car.*

My car was a pre-owned black Mercedes GLK. It wasn't new but it was new to me, and I had purchased it in cash. I kept it spotless and cared for it well; it was a gift from the Lord and I wanted to be a good steward. Now, the Lord was telling me to give it to my then employee. I knew I'd heard God.

A day later, after much prayer, I spoke to my husband Jon about the matter. In typical fashion, Jon pledged to support my obedience to the Lord.

We made the arrangements to ship my car from New York to South Carolina. I paid for the shipping, and felt great peace at blessing my employee with the vehicle.

Not long afterward, that same employee began lying to us. They became dishonorable and disrespectful. Eventually, we caught them stealing as well. In the aftermath, after I'd hired someone else to do their job, I reflected on the fact that I still did not have a car… but they were driving the Mercedes that used to be mine. Still, I had peace, because I knew I'd obeyed the Lord.

Every instance of giving is a seed, and seed produces after its' own kind. Strawberry seeds produce strawberries; avocado seeds produce avocados. And so forth. I had no doubt that my car seed would eventually produce a car.

The *Luke 6:38* principle dictates that when the harvest comes, it comes with upgrade. I didn't know when my car would arrive, but I fully expected it to be better than the one I gave.

I sowed my car in the month of March.

One morning in the month of September, six months later, I distinctly heard the voice of the Lord telling me to go find the car He'd shown me in a dream.

I knew exactly the dream He was talking about, and I remembered that car! A white SUV! I told my husband, "Jon, it's time! It's time for me to receive my car. It's going to be a white SUV!"

To my surprise and delight, Jon made an appointment for us at a Mercedes dealership the very next day. The salesman assigned to greet us met me in the lobby and shook my hand. I noticed his Christian jewelry. He asked me what I did for a living and when I told him I am a minister, he immediately spoke excitedly about his church and faith in Jesus Christ. The term would be, we hit it off! He said, "Do you know what color and make you're looking for?" I said, "A white SUV…?" He told me to wait one moment, he'd be right back.

A few minutes later, the salesman returned and invited me outside. He had taken the liberty of lining up three white SUVs for me to test drive. The moment I got behind the wheel of the one

I would purchase, I knew it was mine. When I wrote the check to purchase it in cash that day, I thanked God… I was driving home a brand new Mercedes GLE, paid in full. The Holy Spirit reminded me of the seed I had sown back in March, and I knew my harvest had come in.

Kingdom Millionaires sow big and we reap big. We hesitate not, and we harvest much.

Kingdom Millionaires are called to navigate assignments and dollar amounts that intimidate others. However, once again, you will find this to be your comfort lane.

We pray big, believe big, ask big, praise big, sow big, reap big, and give all that we can for the Master's uses in the earth, to make a big impact for the wonderful Kingdom of Jesus Christ our Lord! Amen!

DR. JOLYNNE WHITTAKER

Chapter Four

Discernment and Stewardship: Required Tools That Will Multiply Your Money

DR. JOLYNNE WHITTAKER

As one who carries and walks in the wealth anointing, it will be crucial for you to discern the intentions and true spirits of those around you.

Some will seek to gain access to you simply because of the blessing you walk in. Some will want to be connected to you for the benefits they hope you share.

Discernment comes by the Holy Ghost. Discernment, the ability to know, see or sense the truth, is a gift of the Spirit. We know discernment is necessary and highly beneficial simply because it is included in the gifts God gives to men. However, I cannot emphasize enough how much this ability will help you.

People are not always who they pretend to be. Some have become very skilled at presenting a rehearsed and polished version of themselves.

Let the Holy Spirit show you who they really are and what they're really after.

I can tell you, the Lord has always told me the truth about people. I haven't always wanted to believe what the Lord revealed about people, because of course we always hope for the best concerning people. We see their potential and hope they rise to fulfill it. However, every single time God warned me about someone, He was 100% right.

Err on the side of trusting the Lord, always. Regardless of what someone says, promises, or how they present themself, believe what the Lord shows you.

Money attracts people.
Success attracts people.
People are drawn to others who have what they need.

I have had well known Christian ministers take money from me and then stab me in the back. I have seen a major embezzlement in my ministry… at the hands of an employee of another ministry. I have been stolen from by a well-known leader in the Church, and I could go on. Learn from what I am sharing. When God warns you, trust Him. When God tells you to distance yourself from someone, listen to Him.

There will be times God tells you to bless someone. As a matter of fact, the more giving you are and willing to yield in this way to the Holy Spirit, the more God will use you to bless others. This too will multiply your money, because God gives seed to the Sower, not the hoarder.

Yes, many are the times when God has instructed me to give someone a cash blessing. However, there is a stark difference between following the instruction of God, and being a cheerful, generous giver, versus letting someone who is demonically driven, drain you.

Satan despises prosperous believes and he especially hates wealthy believers.
When someone attempts to gain access to you, ask the Lord who sent them.
When someone desires to get close to you, pray and test the spirits. Are they genuine? Do they have an ulterior motive? Are they what I call a serial taker? As sad as it is, there are some who become very comfortable taking from others, and they'll go from person to person, for money.

The Lord impressed upon me the importance of teaching good stewardship. Because yes, the devil will attempt to drain your finances.

Learn to consult the Lord.
Let God direct your giving and investing.
The Lord will send you instructions with confirmations.

If you are confused or conflicted, God is not in it, because there is no confusion in God.

You did not get here by disobeying the voice of God; your obedience, posture and seek, have navigated you to this position of Kingdom wealth. Maintain your position by maintaining your posture.

More is given to the good steward.
Steward well and increase will come quickly and regularly.

This is a strong prophetic word and a compass for your guidance. In the weeks, months and years to come, many will return to this chapter and find confirmation in these words. Glory to Jesus.

I prophesy over you now in the strong and superior name of Jesus Christ our Savior, Lord and King:

God your Heavenly Father has given you eyes to see!
No one shall disguise themselves, fool you, or hide anything from you!

The Lord your God has given you ears to hear!

You will hear the voice of the Holy Spirit and hearken unto His leading!

You will experience peace each time Holy Spirit imparts knowledge to you.

In the name of Jesus!

You have strong discernment in the Holy Ghost! This is one of many spiritual gifting you have, for the Lord has abundantly equipped you for every good work, even for knowing the truth and stewarding your resources. Your discernment is strong and will always reveal the truth, in Jesus' name!

Oh, you are a good steward in the eyes of the Lord, asking for and receiving God's wisdom, living by the Word and reaping the blessings of the Lord! To whom much is given, much is required... and to whom is a good steward, more is given. I prophesy you are on a track of increase to increase, level to level, ever growing and multiplying what God puts in your hand and under your jurisdiction! In the mighty name of **Jesus Christ.**

COME ON AND RECEIVE THAT!
I'm prophesying to you!

Thank you, Jesus.
Bless your people, increase your people, do it for your glory and your Kingdom's sake!

DR. JOLYNNE WHITTAKER

Chapter Five

You Will Encounter Explosive Increase

DR. JOLYNNE WHITTAKER

As someone who is called to the Millionaire Realm, you will walk in a financial anointing, which means you will soon become comfortable navigating the realm of explosive increase.

This path is known for its high intensity, Kingdom-level, inventive and consistent, supernatural and often strategic, *explosive increase*.

Even now, as you begin the journey of reading this book, I bless you in the name of Jesus. I call you protected and prospered, all the days of your life. May the King be glorified by the anointing on your life. May your anointing take you to places higher than anything you never dreamed of, and may the joy of the Lord always be your strength. May you walk in supernatural health as you navigate your financial anointing. Yes, and may your gift always make room for you, even as you go from glory to glory in Christ Jesus. Hallelujah!

Receive that, in Jesus' name!
And now, let me teach you some secrets regarding explosive increase.

Many believe increase just happens, but it does not. Increase is provoked.

The Bible reveals God will give seed to the Sower, He will promote the one who is excellent within their assignment/position, and He will give more to the one who multiplies what He gives them.

Read that again and let the Lord minister to you.

I've watched people brush off or minimize those principles again and again, and foolishly so. God's millionaires do not do so. Each person I've met or mentored who carries a significant financial anointing, (1) is a strong and consistent Sower, (2) strives toward personal excellence on a continual basis, and (3) works to increase what God has already given them.

I have observed these things often come naturally to many Kingdom Millionaires. It's just in them to do these things. Some have to be taught or willing to learn these principles, but the key is that they are willing. The unwilling cannot be taught, and the untaught are not principled. Those who refuse to honor and live by the principles of God, cannot hope to live under an Open Heaven.

Here is another truth:

Many in the body of Christ think size doesn't matter, amounts don't matter, impact doesn't matter. Such people believe and often say, "only the posture of your heart matters". The truth is, all those things matter to the Lord. We surely must have the correct heart posture towards King Jesus: a posture of surrender, holiness, integrity and reverence.

The correct heart posture toward God also includes caring about what *He* cares about. What does God care about the most? The scriptures reveal that best:

John 3:16 -- For God so loved the world, that he gave his only begotten Son, that whosoever believeth in him should not perish, but have everlasting life.

2 Peter 3:9 -- The Lord is not slack concerning his promise, as some men count slackness; but is longsuffering to us-ward, not willing that any should perish, but that all should come to repentance.

Matthew 28:19-20 -- Go ye therefore, and teach all nations, baptizing them in the name of the Father, and of the Son, and of the Holy Ghost: Teaching them to observe all things whatsoever I have commanded you: and, lo, I am with you always, even unto the end of the world. Amen.

John 21:17 -- He saith unto him the third time, Simon, son of Jonas, lovest thou me? Peter was grieved because he said unto him the third time, Lovest thou me? And he said unto him, Lord, thou knowest all things; thou knowest that I love thee. Jesus saith unto him, Feed my sheep.

From these verses, we see the clear truth: God loves people. God cares about people. God wants to help lost people. God wants us to share Jesus so people can be saved. God desires no flesh to perish. God gave His only begotten Son, the Lord Jesus Christ, for the salvation and reconciliation, of Him to people!

So when we talk about you carrying a financial anointing, be sure God is going to call you to help or impact… you guessed it, people.

Yes, your anointing will be to bless you. Yes, because you are willing and obedient, you will eat the good of the land. Yes, your wealth will empower you to leave an inheritance for your children. Yes, your wealth is to make you the head and not the tail. Your wealth is to make you above only, and never beneath. Your wealth will set you apart, set you on high, and it will cause wealth, treasures, and riches to be in your home, which is as it should be, because you are a child of the King; you were made to live royal, always royal, never low.

But do not be naive; the Kingdom Ambassador with significant wealth will be expected to bless and help others. The Kingdom Millionaire will be expected to fund the Kingdom Agenda.

And as you get involved with what God cares about, He'll get involved with what you care about. When you build God's house and commit to His directives, He'll build your house and come behind you to prosper the work of your hands.

Yet make no mistake, and I say this prophetically: God wants you to do big things. God wants you to think big and flow big. He wants you to believe big, pray big, ask big and receive the big.

For simply put, a successful business produces more blessing and opportunity for yourself and others, as opposed to a struggling one.

A thriving and continually increasing, Holy Ghost-anointed ministry saves more souls and impacts lives more greatly, as opposed to a stagnant ministry or church.

If this offends you, perhaps you're not ready for explosive increase, because an effective Kingdom Millionaire must have the humility and fortitude, to see things the way God sees them.

We are operating within the framework of a dark, wicked, dying world that desperately needs Jesus. Time is running out and we have work to do. There are operations to build, movements to launch, families to impact, regions to influence, cities to take back! There are spheres of influence to influence and Kingdom projects to fund. The Millionaire Anointing is on the rise for these reasons!

Then there's this: healthy, supernatural, blessed, and wealthy, is simply who we are. It's who we're *supposed* to be. Read *Deuteronomy 28:1-14* and let the Lord show you. Know those verses well and understand they are God's promises to you. Those promises produce a strong, wealthy servant of the Lord, there's just no two ways about it! Use that anointed passage of scripture as a response to the nay sayers that inevitably come.

Well, let them say what they like, but we have an example to set. We have a message to deliver. We are called to live as the head and not the tail. We are called to live blessed because the Lord has made us rich and added no painful toil or sorrow to it. This is a powerful secret to explosive increase: I'm talking about clarity in your identity and the refusal to denounce or minimize it!

You see, whether God places you as a voice of leadership in your family or a person of influence in an industry or region, you are there to impact things for Jesus. Having big resources and big prosperity, will facilitate that.

How many very well-meaning Christians have been shut down, toyed with by the devil, or outright stopped, because they did not have the resources to do what God told them to do?

I have known Christians who have wanted to do things for the poor, for the homeless, for the forgotten and disdained of society, such as the abused or the addict. If those Christians had the resources they needed, they wouldn't have been delayed or shut down.

I have known Christians who have a vision for a ministry, movement, or business, something they know the Lord told them to do. I have been on the receiving end of frantic phone calls or text messages, where a minister is asking for financial assistance because they are in an urgent situation... again. It would be far better for that minister to get a revelation of true, holy Biblical prosperity, and learn the secrets to explosive increase, so they can flow in Kingdom wealth and grow in their Kingdom assignment!

A Kingdom Millionaire can provide answers and resources in a crisis.
God's Kingdom Millionaires can be a blessing to their family, their church, their community. Their lives are shining examples of the abundance of God; they don't just talk it, they walk it, they live it!

A Kingdom Millionaire will not open up a Go-Fund-Me or take up special offerings for several months in order to do something God has laid on their heart. They are empowered and equipped to simply *do* what God tells them to do. What a difference! What Kingdom order! What

Kingdom power, style and flawless execution! And yet…

This has become an area of contention and argument for many, because the thought that a thriving ambassador can be more immediately effective than a struggling ambassador, offends people. Why does it offend them? Only because they take it as a personal judgement rather than a prophetic word with the capacity to lift them to a greater level.

It's pride. I'm calling it out.
It's also small thinking. Let's call that out, too.

Of course a small, anointed and blessed movement, business or ministry can be impactful. Of course it can! Nevertheless, the greater the movement, the more impactful it will be.

The first secret to explosive increase, is knowing God wants you to increase explosively! Any obstacle you can think of, can be removed by the Lord. Any deficit that comes to mind concerning you, God can strengthen and help you with.

I prophesy God wants you to grow, and you shall grow!

Like Isaac and the early Church, God wants you to wax great, and you shall indeed wax very great! In the mighty name of Jesus Christ!
-- *Genesis 26:13, Acts 2:47, Acts 16:5, Proverb 10:22*

You know, this truth is also controversial for some people because they don't want to feel as though they're not doing enough. In reality, each man and woman must find his or her lane, being led of the Lord. In your lane, be content and complete. Hallelujah!

It's ok if someone is not called to the Kingdom Millionaire lane; it's perfectly ok if the Lord places them elsewhere or uses them otherwise.

But let's not trash the higher flyers! There is an eagle realm that has been ordained and blessed by the Lord. Just because someone is not called to fly within that sphere, why try to throw rocks at the eagles?

Doing so is self destructive behavior, and counterproductive to the body of Christ. See that. And while we're looking at this truth, let me prophetically remind you, a house divided upon itself cannot stand. We know that, and so does the devil. Let's not let that defeated foe divide and weaken us!

If I could stand before such individuals, I would say:

Humble yourself. Get into the presence of God and get a revelation of Kingdom wealth. Learn the principles. Let the Master teach you. For you will be amazingly and wonderfully more impactful than ever before, and it will happen quickly — if you will stop being offended by the truth!

And the truth is: God does not desire you to remain in the days of humble beginnings, forever. God desires you to increase and impact, for the glory and purposes of Jesus Christ our King!

Now let me talk to *you*, Kingdom Millionaire. Here is what you need to know now, regarding your imminent explosive increase - and I pray you receive this in Jesus' name! The following are secrets to explosive increase, and these secrets are for you.

Increase, passion and greatness in the Kingdom produces great impact. Let this be your goal. How will you provoke increase? By pursuing and functioning in excellence, consistently. By diligently seeking God and never growing lukewarm. Don't let it happen! Stay hot! Stay on fire! Stay in His presence! As you do… you will take on the glorious glow of the Lord, just like Moses did, and you will hunger for the things *He* hungers for: a massive harvest of souls in a dying world! Stay lit in the Holy Ghost and hungry to fulfill your Assignment from the Lord; this will ensure God provides you with every resource you'll ever need.

The Lord desires every man and every woman to aspire to the highest possible position and performance within their assignment, blessing or sphere of influence. Make this your mindset and your goal, while maintaining humility, and you will fly high indeed! Jesus modeled this for us eloquently in *Luke 4:1-13* when Satan tempted Him, then later in *Matthew 26:53* when He allowed Himself to be taken into custody unjustly. Jesus knew His identity, He knew the resources He had at His fingertips, yet He remained strong in His assignment and allegiance to the Kingdom Agenda.

For you, this will take humility, strength, spiritual maturity and loyalty to Jesus above all else. Never forget these words. Allegiance to the Kingdom above all else, shunning the fear of man at all costs, will position you for great use, every time.

With great use will come the need for great strength and any resources required; Jehovah Jireh will always provide. You will go, you will grow, you will increase, you will wax great, and you will be impactful for the Lord — because of your excellent spirit, humble heart and fierce faith. Glory to God!

Has the Lord shown you a level that is above where you are now? Be honest with yourself, because God knows you saw what He showed you!

This is your sign that increase draws nigh!

This is your confirmation that you may not always be able, but God is always able, and His strength will be made perfect in your weaknesses. Lean on Jesus and watch Him give victory every time!

This is your sign to believe in you… because God does. This is most definitely your sign to believe what God told you can be yours and go for it!

You have no idea how God will increase you as you obey the last command He gave you.

You have no idea how explosive your next level will be, simply because you had the faith to trust God in this season.

Some people don't want to take risks and some don't want to do the work related to real destiny. I'm not kidding, I've heard and seen it! But you are ready to grow, and so you shall. You are trusting the Lord, and so you will see Him increase and use you exponentially. You are ready to roll up your sleeves and do what God called you to do, and that is why He will explosively increase you at a speed that simply blows your mind! Receive that in Jesus' name!

Oh, I pray somebody hears what I'm saying by the Holy Ghost: if you are grateful and yet divinely discontent where you are, that's a sign God is about to open up something greater to you.

At this point, many reading this book are feeling a stirring in your spirit. You're ready to step into a season of elevation that leads to a lifetime of explosive increase in the Lord!

Christ Jesus is putting a demand on your anointing.
The Spirit of God is stirring your heart toward destiny.
In the name of the Lord, I prophesy over you now, the Master has need of you!

Surely this is your moment to step into position for such a time as this!

I speak explosive increase over you in the name of Jesus!

Receive God's decree from *Ephesians 3:20:*

Now unto Him that is able to do exceedingly abundantly above all that we ask or think, according to the power that worketh in us — you shall now go and grow, and rise and go higher in the mighty name of Jesus Christ our King!

As you enter into this position in the Kingdom, you will begin to receive wisdom and instructions from the Lord.

God will tell you how to expand and multiply what He gives you.

Obey the Lord. In your obedience, I prophesy you will receive MORE! In the mighty name of Jesus!

May you ever stay close to the Giver of your Destiny, hallelujah!
May Jesus ever be the Master of your life!

May wealth and riches ever be in your home, and may the wisdom of God be the compass that guides you both day and night. May the Holy Spirit speak to you with clarity and may you pursue, subdue, attain and fulfill everything He tells you, in Jesus' name!

We need you here, Kingdom Millionaire.
We need your spirit and your fire, in Jesus' name!
We need your boldness and your tenacity.
We need your example and your excellence.
Your story and your destiny will be a path for others to walk… and they too will rise. In the name of Jesus!

The body of Christ needs who you are and what God has put upon your life.
The body of Christ needs you strong in your assignment, a shining example of God's goodness.

I speak excellent health and length of days over you, in Jesus' name!

I speak vision and provision and alignment for every assignment, in Jesus' name!

I declare you are here for such a time as this, may the Lord protect, prosper and propel you to heights and destinations you never dreamed! And may your testimony be a roadmap for others to find victory in Christ, even as your Millionaire Anointing be of impact and influence in every room and realm Jesus leads you to.

Godspeed and God bless you!

May your life be a shining gem in the Master's hand, may your legacy be for the glory of Christ Jesus and His Kingdom! May you ever be healthy and whole, great and strong, purposeful and prosperous, in Jesus' name!

DR. JOLYNNE WHITTAKER

Chapter Six

Supernatural Secrets That Open Doors

DR. JOLYNNE WHITTAKER

I encourage you to never think you have 'arrived'. Don't let complacency seep in, it's a killer of dreams. By becoming complacent or feeling accomplished and finished, many miss what God has next. Stay hungry!

Don't ever sit down. Don't ever become too satisfied. There is always more in God! Stay on your path, stay in the ring! Stay in the game, and be in it to win it! I assure you, no one will reach millionaire or multi-millionaire status in the Lord, if they are complacent and not on fire with the pursuit of their destiny.

I have learned God will surprise you just when you think you've seen it all. I've learned He will reveal new paths and pursuits, He'll open up new vistas, just when you get comfortable and confident at the level you're in.

So as you stay in pursuit of the Lord your God and all He has for your life... I urge you to also stay ready! I feel to prophesy now in the strong name of Jesus: More good things are coming for you! Something new is coming for you! God has another level, a fresh assignment for you! Receive that now in Jesus' mighty name.

The Lord is highly strategic and very organized. He knew you would be reading this book on this day, at this precise time. He knows, after all, the end from the beginning. So as I realize God knew you would find yourself reading these words on this very page, I feel confident to say, this is your sign that another level is coming for your life. This world needs more Spirit-filled, faith-filled, fierce and on fire Christians, *like you!*

I prophesy this is your time to do a new thing in God's will! You are not a common person, nor were you ever. You have always been unique and unusual, just the way God made you. Hallelujah! And so in the strong name of Jesus, I prophesy this is your time to receive unique and unusual elevation into something fresh and impactful, in Jesus' name!

I have noticed many of the people who prosper significantly in the Lord, are called to impact their family or community, often both. Many people who God leads to read this book, will be positioned in strategic places or in proximity to individuals they are assigned to impact for Jesus.

You are called to shift the atmospheres.
You are called to enter and dominate God-ordained rooms.
You are called to infiltrate, influence and occupy God-ordained realms.
You are called to be rich so your money can magnify the name of Jesus.

Many of you are called to fund and finance the Kingdom Agenda *and* significant projects according to the will and plan of God. And so in Jesus' name I say, *Godspeed! Pursue! Go forth boldly and successfully, be influential and blessed, for the glory of Jesus!*

Your consistency and hunger will function as supernatural keys that open doors for you.

I personally believe Joseph's story of uncommon persistence and consistence in his faith, despite unthinkable betrayals, opposition and attacks, is a strong message to Kingdom Ambassadors today: don't be naive, the devil will try to come for you.

He will try to cause things that destroy, depress and deter you. But if you'll stay consistent and hungry in the Lord, ever growing in your faith and spiritual authority, ever bowed low in submission and reverence at the feet of Jesus, you will gain a reputation as someone demons don't want to mess with!

Do you remember that situation with the seven sons of Sceva? My goodness, that account provides prophetic insight that I liken unto pure gold!

From that account we learn, there is a place you can get in your spiritual position and authority, that makes demons nervous. They'll think twice about attacking you. Warnings will go out concerning you: *Don't mess with that one, you won't get anywhere and they retaliate! Hey, don't meddle or attack that one, Jesus really loves them so He'll send combat angels!*

It will become known and understood that you are a true warrior for Christ! Hey, this isn't like the old days, when you were easily intimidated or rattled by the demonic. This isn't like your early days as a Christian, when your exousia was immature and you did not yet have a measure of Dunamis and faith. Now, you are a force to be reckoned with! Now, hell will be shaken if they make you mad! Yes, because you'll pray the kind of prayers that stop devils in their tracks! You'll stand strong in the Lord and the power of His might and Heavenly angels will come to fight on your behalf! Wheww, you are an anointed Kingdom Millionaire, enemies of God better watch out!

In that famous Bible account involving the seven sons of Sceva and the apostle Paul, we learn the reality of spiritual authority. Some have it and some don't, and the demons know who is who.

Some people are easily slapped around by the devil - and too often, quite literally. That's what happened to the Jewish exorcists in *Acts 19:11-16*.

They were verbally assaulted by a man with demons, then physically accosted. When the would-be exorcists tried to cast the demon out, the unholy spirit had the audacity to talk back! Why? Because it could. There was no authority in the room to silence it, much less cast it out.

The inexperienced and ill-equipped sons of Sceva said, "*I adjure you by the Jesus whom Paul proclaims…*"

The demon actually replied and said, *Jesus I know, and Paul I recognize, but who are you?*

Imagine! *Acts 19:16-17* says that devil proceeded to strip the would-be exorcists naked and beat their butts. They ran out of the house terrified and terrorized, and word spread about what had happened to them.

Imagine their embarrassment. But the Lord took what the devil meant for evil and turned it for good, as He often does. Instead of word spreading about how powerful the demon was, word spread concerning Jesus, and the name of Jesus was extolled!

People who had been practicing divination and sorcery, imagining they were spiritually safe or somehow pleasing to God, came forth and denounced their beliefs and practices. Then they burned their books. Word of the Lord Jesus Christ increased and prevailed mightily.
—*Acts 19:18-20*

Here is your take-away:

Spiritual authority can be recognized.
Spiritual authority paralyzes hell and decimates demonic agendas.
Spiritual authority is developed.
Spiritual authority is developed as you remain consistent and hungry in your pursuit of Jesus.
Authority in the spirit is necessary.

Without authority in the spirit, you will not be equipped to address and overcome situations and attempted attacks that arise. To the contrary, being one who carries weight in the spirit, deflects and breaks attacks before they even begin!

Put yourself on the path to go higher in your authority, today! Make it your aim to be consistent in the Lord. Labor in the Word. Maintain your prayer and worship life. Praise your way into His presence and bask in the glory that fills the atmosphere. Maintain your posture of obedience and excellence, never let it slip! These things position you to be a powerful overcomer in the body of Christ. Amen?

As a prophet I say to you today:
If you're going to carry a financial anointing, you will surely need authority and weight in the spirit. This will protect and insulate you. This will also open uncommon doors unto you!

Stay hungry, child of God. Do not eat from the lavish table God lays before you, then become full and complacent in your prosperity. Stay hungry! Please consider and meditate on the strong warning found here:

Deuteronomy 8:7-18
For the Lord your God is bringing you into a good land—a land with brooks, streams, and deep springs gushing out into the valleys and hills; a land with wheat and barley, vines and fig trees, pomegranates, olive oil and honey; a land where bread will not be scarce and you will lack nothing; a land where the rocks are iron and you can dig copper out of the hills.

When you have eaten and are satisfied, praise the Lord your God for the good land he has given you. Be careful that you do not forget the Lord your God, failing to observe his commands, his laws and his decrees that I am giving you this day. Otherwise, when you eat and are satisfied, when you build fine houses and settle down, and when your herds and flocks grow large and your silver and gold increase and all you have is multiplied, then your heart will become proud and you will forget the Lord your God, who brought you out of Egypt, out of the land of slavery. He led you through the vast and dreadful wilderness, that thirsty and waterless land, with its venomous snakes and scorpions. He brought you water out of hard rock.

He gave you manna to eat in the wilderness, something your ancestors had never known, to humble and test you so that in the end it might go well with you. You may say to yourself,

"My power and the strength of my hands have produced this wealth for me." But remember the Lord your God, for it is he who gives you the ability to produce wealth, and so confirms his covenant, which he swore to your ancestors, as it is today.

Many people become satisfied, then complacent.
Many believe, achieve, receive, then wrongly
assume they have arrived at the highest level.
No, there is always more in God.
There is always another realm for you to access.
The contingency? Your obedience and reverence,
always. Never let it wane!

—*2 Corinthians 3:18, Hebrews 11:6*

As I close this chapter, I feel led of the Lord to declare to you: a major supernatural key that will open major doors for you, is your ability to see and believe for the BIG.

God is a big God who wants to do big things in the earth! The Lord is looking for people who are hungry to be used as tools in His mighty hand. Is that you? Are you ready for this?

Believe for the mega and the power of divine providence. For in the mighty name of Jesus I say, there is increase and great destiny coming to your life in the season to come! Glory to God!

DR. JOLYNNE WHITTAKER

Chapter Seven

A Massive Wealth Transfer Is Coming

DR. JOLYNNE WHITTAKER

A massive wealth transfer is coming and nothing can stop it.

I have said this several times on our television programs and online, but the Lord made it very clear that it needs to be in print as well. Speaking the word of the Lord allows people to point to a place and date when God said something and later did it; this brings Him glory.

So let's go.

For more years than the average person wants to know about, wicked people have been engaged in an organized effort to steal money, funds, resources, land and wealth from others. These efforts have been well planned, organized, executed, and very successful.

I could mention the pharmaceutical industry, which has deliberately created drugs that are addictive and harmful, drugs that perpetuate sickness and thus the need for medical care. Drug companies have never been in business to get people well; they've been in cahoots to keep people sick, in order to keep the very big business of big Pharma, thriving.

Doctors are offered lucrative gifts and deals for pushing certain drugs to their patients. The wooing of docs begins in medical school, where the practice of wining and dining the soon to be credentialed medial students, begins. True healing restores and liberates a person; the medical industry seeks to enslave a person. This is widely known now, but it didn't used to be.

And so, think of the medial practices, doctors, drug companies, pharmacies and insurance companies, that have made mega bucks… Think of the concerted push to silence and degrade natural healing modalities and practitioners, such as nutritionists and naturopathic doctors.

What is going on? Well it's concerted theft, the result of which is an un-authorized wealth transfer, as people pay doctor bills, the fees for insurance plans, and buy untold amounts of medicines over the course of their lifetime. It's highway robbery, when natural health practices keep a person healthy, because the body is fearfully and wonderfully made, able to renew, regenerate and restore itself.

Yet, because humans are in a fallen world and condition, the Lord saw to it that divine healing was provided and made available to us, by the sacrificial Blood of Jesus and the sending of His Word.

Sickness is big business and has been the means for unholy wealth transfers, for many, many years.
—*Psalm 139:14, 1 Peter 2:24, Psalm 107:20*

I could mention the baby formula industry, which convinced mothers that their product was better for their baby's health, when in fact any honest OB-GYN or pediatric doctor, would vehemently tell you otherwise. The product was marketed to be better, healthier, and more reliable that mother's milk, and it was coined a relief and convenience for moms who could not or chose not, to nurse. Untold babies worldwide were deprived of the immunities, nutrition and God-created benefits of mother's milk… and those industries made trillions of dollars.

I could go to yet another example - how about one of the most recent, the pandemic? Orchestrated and planned many years in advance by globalists and so-called elite families of the world, the worldwide pandemic of 2020-2021 resulted in the loss of jobs, business and properties, for people all over the world.

Many could not work, businesses were forced to close, and people lost their homes. Many, under the pressure and fear, lost their minds. Psychiatric and counseling services skyrocketed in demand. The hand-sanitizer, PVC and mask industries boomed, and let's not get started on what companies like Pfizer and Moderna, made.

I recall seeing a boat-tour of a super-yacht that had, of all things, an actual laboratory on board!

The reason was because its' owner was one of the scientists who helped engineer pandemic "product" for big Pharma. As a yacht enthusiast, I knew exactly what that vessel must have cost, and my mind was blown. Covid-Billionaires and Covid-Trillionaires are now real terms, while for the average person that time was a season of anything but success and wealth. What were they doing? Well, it was a well-planned un-authorized wealth transfer and land grab, in preparation of (hopefully) creating the scenario required to usher in the one world order.

What does God say about wicked people who rob from others to make themselves rich?

What does the Bible say, if anything, about what happens to those who willfully oppress others in order to benefit themselves?

Ohhh, God has a lot to say!

You see, there is nothing new under the sun. Money and power have always been intoxicating for some.

The Word says the love of money is the root of all evil, and we only need to consider the above very few examples, to substantiate that scripture. God never lies. The unholy blood-thirst for mega wealth, has always been the driving force behind evil practices and agendas. As Pharaoh in Egypt, displayed so astutely. —*1 Timothy 6:10*

Pharaoh was happy to oppress, abuse and enslave the Israelites for the purpose of enjoying a free workforce that gave Egypt a booming economy.

But the Israelites were God's people, and when Jehovah had enough, it all came crashing down! —*Exodus 6:5*

Pharaoh was first terrorized by the living God, as the Lord made an open mockery of Egypt's false demonic 'gods' and established Himself holy and sovereign over all. —*Exodus 6:1, Exodus 11:1,8*

Then Pharaoh was forced to comply with God's demand to let His people go… but not without retribution and recompense for all they had suffered. Not without justice being served. Pharaoh had made unholy money off the Israelites; now Pharaoh had to surrender the goods to God's people! —*Exodus 12:31*

In a stunning example of an Authorized Wealth Transfer, that is, one that is sanctioned by God, Moses instructed the Israelites to ask the Egyptians for what they wanted. In return the Egyptians surrendered all their best and most expensive goods to God's people. —*Exodus 12:36*

Such a wealth transfer is coming again.

The wicked, worshiping Mammon, have stored up unholy mega wealth.

But the Lord, will yank that unauthorized wealth out of those wicked hands, and washing it all in the Blood of Jesus (the ultimate righteous way to do money laundering, come on somebody!) God will give money, which is a neutral commodity and can be used for much good by righteous people, to His people.

A major, mega, massive God-ordained transfer of wealth is coming to the Church of Jesus Christ, and all I can say is, *Get Ready!*

We know God cannot give us something we cannot handle.
We know the Lord, as a Good Father, cannot put a blessing into unholy hands.

Stay pure.
Stay holy.
Stay in position.
Stay ready!
Display good stewardship; let God *see* you're ready to receive!

To the best of your ability, seek and utilize God's wisdom, as found in the Holy Bible. To the best of your ability, obey the Word at all times. When the soon-coming wealth transfer begins, it is going to come to the ones who are ready. It will be given to the ones who are found obedient and capable. Your obedience and capability to handle, steward, interact with, multiply, distribute and utilize wealth, will also determine the amount you are given. Please, please, oh please read that again.

We have all read or heard about, the stories where someone poor wins the lottery, or perhaps it's someone with no experience managing money well. A person who wants the money, but has no personal discipline or Godly standard by which they live. Time and time again, that person ends up lost, destitute, strung out on drugs, or right back where they started with no money.

What happened? In many cases, they blew it all quickly. They bought houses for all their family members, bought all the things they'd always wanted to have, or maybe they drank or gambled it away. Time and again we hear these heart-breaking stories. What happened? Someone who was not prepared, disciplined or capable, came into wealth. Without the spiritual foundation and skillset to manage it well, they lost it.

This cannot be you. God wants to develop you now, for what is coming. God wants to see you cultivate the habits and Biblical literacy now, to manage well.

I hear the Lord saying He desires to shake loose the unauthorized wealth of the wicked and give it to the just! In this season, the Lord is looking not just for the hands that go up to receive their portion, but the hands who reach for what is theirs in both wisdom and prudence. Selah. Hear what I'm saying by the Spirit of God! Glory to Jesus forevermore.

Proverb 15:6
There is treasure in the house of the godly,
but the earnings of the wicked bring trouble. (NLT)

Isaiah 1:19
If you are willing and obedient, you will
eat the good things of the land… (NIV)

Proverb 13:22
A good man leaveth an inheritance to his children's
children:and the wealth of the sinner is
laid up for the just. (KJV)

Ecclesiastes 2:26
To the person who pleases him, God gives wisdom, knowledge and happiness, but to the sinner he gives the task of gathering and storing up wealth to hand it over to the one who pleases God. (NIV)

I want you to take a moment and go prayerfully before the Lord; let Him minister to you about the above scriptures. Let the Holy Spirit help you process and understand exactly what the Lord is saying. Because I assure you, He says only what He means, and He meant exactly what He said.

Godly people are destined to have treasure in their homes. This is the will and the way of the Lord. By God's design, a well-appointed home is your destiny. In addition, all of the good things this earth yields to eat; all of the beautiful and valuable treasures made by the Lord, were made for His people, not the wicked of the earth.

It is God's will for you to eat the good of the land, not the ungodly. The exchange required for this blessing, is that you must be willing and obedient. The good of the land means the best earth has to offer.

While you occupy on earth until King Jesus comes again, the Lord wants you to have an inheritance mindset, because He has given scriptural provision for you to prosper to the extent that you are able to leave an inheritance to your children, even your grand-children. A part of the means by which you will do so, is by receiving wealth that is transferred to *you*, from sinners.

All of that is incredible and mind blowing! What a God! What a Mighty Heavenly Father! What a Good God! Now grasp this: as I type these words for you to read, and as you hold this book in your hands and read it, there are ungodly people, some of them very wicked, storing up massive wealth and they're in for a surprise. Unbeknownst to them, the Lord they shun has given them the job of gathering and storing up wealth… only to hand it over to the people who please God, at the appointed time.

Kingdom Millionaire, I prophesy again in the mighty name of Jesus Christ our King: There is coming a massive wealth transfer into the body of Christ, and nothing in this world can stop it. GET READY! I said Get Ready - Get Ready - GET READY!

DR. JOLYNNE WHITTAKER

Chapter Eight

The Wealth Anointing Is A Power Position
(And Power Must Be Properly Placed)

DR. JOLYNNE WHITTAKER

More than any other book I've written to date, it was made clear to me that Prophetic Words for Kingdom Millionaires is a much-needed book in the body of Christ.

A foundational resource for understanding and receiving the prophetic words in *this* book, is my previous work, *Stepping Into Favor* and its subsequent intensive resource, *It's Time To Soar*. These are two best-sellers the Lord used me to write in 2017-2019. Without a foundational and working understanding of the favor and financial principles God has given us in the Holy Bible, one cannot successfully access and occupy the millionaire realm. Please note: accessing, and occupying this realm, are two completely different things. Yes Lord, let us access this position, but please develop in us the heart, tenacity and power required, to remain there!

Furthermore, as I wrote this book, the Lord impressed upon me *Prophetic Words for Kingdom Millionaires* is a book the enemy hoped would never get into your hands. Some messages from the Lord serve as prophetic activation and impartations, all glory to God!

On the flip-side, *Prophetic Words for Kingdom Millionaires* is a book that will be kept from the hands of some. Why is that? Simply put, many will want the millionaire anointing, but not everyone should have it. Some who genuinely want it, will not attain or occupy it. Like a wise mother keeps her child from touching a hot stove, I believe God will keep this door closed to some.

I realize this may be hard for some to understand. Let me show you something. Please pay attention very carefully.

In *Ephesians 3:20,* we learn that the fullness of God is able to do exceedingly abundantly above all that we ask or think, *according to the power that works in us.*

In *Acts 1:8*, we learn this power comes from the Holy Ghost. When the Holy Ghost comes upon us, we receive power. Yes, and subsequent verses reveal what this power does or produces:

boldness, heavenly tongues which facilitate secure and supernaturally encoded conversations with Heaven, scriptural understanding and literacy, activation into destiny.

Wow. No wonder this power is required to get wealth:

> *Deuteronomy 8:18*
> *But thou shat remember the lord thy*
> *God: for it is He that giveth thee*
> *power to get wealth, the He may establish*
> *His covenant which He sware unto*
> *thy fathers, as it is this day.*

Wow again. So power is required to get wealth (since the devil isn't going to handle it over willingly, nor will the assignments that come with wealth, be a cake-walk: for the Bible says, *To whom much is given much is required.* Wow yet again. — Luke 12:48

Yes. Indeed. Wow, Lord. Thank You Father, for this deep revelation. Wealth is attained by power. That power comes from the Holy Ghost. That power is obtained and increased by our pursuit in the Lord. Hallelujah. That power goes hand in hand with authority (Dunamis and Exousia) and it is that authority demons both recognize and fear.

Oh, yes! And that same power facilitates the level to which You can work in us, O God. And it is that same power that comes with the anointing that destroys yokes … which means occupying this power position comes with Breaker Anointing capabilities… by which we will see deliverance take place, divine doors fly open, demonic doors nailed shut, bondages destroyed and acquisitions come forth.

Make the connection.
Draw lines between these dots.

This is crucial and expedient for anyone who will stand in the position of a Kingdom Millionaire. Thank You, Jesus.

It is required that you know your source, your reality, your identity, what God requires of you, and what this anointing on your life can do. Speak, Jesus. Open our hearts and minds. Use us for Your glory. Anoint us to walk this path for You, dear Jesus.

And so, let us prophetically connect the dots: The common denominator for wealth… deliverance… impact… command of the Word… authority in the spirit… position and occupation of destiny… boldness and faith… is DUNAMIS, or power.

Does everyone have it?
No, every Christian does not have it.

Can anyone develop and receive it?
Yes, any Christian who is willing to pursue, can receive. And yes, a select number will… while many won't.

For this reason, I now understand the reasons this book was fought… and fortified. I understand why it was a target… and why it is a tool!

Oh, glory to God! I speak health and wealth over you in the mighty name of Jesus! I speak boldness and growth over you now, in Jesus' name! I decree and declare this is a set time for you. This is a destiny moment for you.

This very moment is a divine appointment for you and I say in the matchless and superior name of Jesus, arise, Kingdom Millionaire! Arise and get ready to be deployed in the army of the Lord! Get ready to see things you've never seen before! Get ready to do things you've never done! Get ready to live burning for Jesus and ablaze with the glory as an Ambassador for Christ in the earth! *Receive in Jesus' name!*

DR. JOLYNNE WHITTAKER

Chapter Nine

The Power of Prophetic Words and Instructions

DR. JOLYNNE WHITTAKER

Again and again, I return to the Biblical accounts of Naman, the widow in debt, and Elisha.

Both of these iconic Biblical accounts reveal the gravity and power of a true prophetic word and an anointed prophetic instruction.

I go so far as to say these accounts are solid gold, ready to be mined by the one with discernment and hunger. Is that you?

Here, we learn that not every word spoken by every person, is the same. Anointed vessels of the Lord release prophetic power when they speak the will of God. That prophetic power, encapsulated in their words, can bring forth miracles.

This is folly to the worldly mind, and it is unattainable to the dishonorable believer, but to a follower of Jesus who both recognizes and honors a prophetic vessel speaking prophetic words, what blessings that person can attain from a prophetic word or instruction spoken in season!

Let me show you something. The Lord taught me this many years ago. Imagine: your words carry power. Your own words are infused with the very breath of God. His breath in your lungs, gives your words creative power.

Which of course makes sense, because you were made in the image of God, therefore you have His characteristics and attributes. Well, God is a Master Creator, indeed a Creative Genius, who created the world on which we live, in just six days. He did so by speaking. Hence we say, God spoke the worlds into existence. Hallelujah! God did so easily and flawlessly, because His very words are saturated with creative power. When God speaks, the elements He created must activate and respond, according to the commands of their Creator.
—*Genesis 1:1-27*

See the gravity of this. Speech has power. Beings made in the image of God, emit traces of God's power in their speech. That's why our words have power to create outcomes and speak things into existence. Life and death are in the power of the tongue, even blessing and cursing,

according to *Proverb 18:21 and James 3:10*. That's how we're able to call forth those things that be not, and see what we've spoken weave itself into form - pulled from the spirit into the natural!
—*Romans 4:17*

Now see this: Words uttered at the command of the Lord, by an anointed and appointed Prophet of God, create outcomes, breakthroughs and miracles on a supernatural level! Because the prophet is speaking at the instruction of the Lord, speaking the will and words of the Lord, utilizing the anointing they carry within the mantle they wear... which causes supernatural things to happen in real time!

When the esteemed army officer Naaman realized his leprosy was not going to improve, but rather kill him, Naaman knew he had to do something. Unwilling to die a slow, sure, painful and inevitable death, Naaman also knew he could not hide his disease for long. Rotting flesh emits a most foul, unmistakable odor; falling-off extremities and digits cannot be hidden or disguised. How long could Naaman hide his condition? Here was a man of position and prosperity, a man of influence and affluence in the community, but none of that could save Naaman. However, in Naaman's household was an Israelite slave girl. This girl knew her God could heal Naaman of his leprosy, and she knew Elisha the prophet, would be the point of contact for the healing power of the Lord to flow forth.

But as we read this jaw-dropping account in *2 Kings 5:1-19*, we learn something fascinating.

Sometimes it's not only a prophetic word that is needed.

Sometimes, there are instructions to follow.

Sometimes, the individual in need must put their faith into action.

Sometimes there are requirements to be met and possibly, just possibly, meeting those requirements satisfies the principles outlined in *James 2:26* (faith without works is dead) and *Hebrews 11:6* (God rewards those who diligently seek Him).

There is always a portion for the one who will go out on a limb... as the vertically challenged (short!) tax collector Zacchaeus found out in *Luke 19:1-10*. If Zacchaeus had not taken the initiative to climb up a tree so he could see Jesus passing by, he would not have gained the attention of the King... which resulted in redemption for Zacchaeus and salvation for his house.

Such was the case for Naaman.

In this fascinating Biblical lesson, we learn the power of (1) receiving a genuine prophetic word and (2) releasing our faith by following any prophetic instruction that comes with the word.

With nothing to lose and everything to gain, desperate for answers and willing to go for it, Naaman packs himself up and sets off to find Elisha, with gifts and offerings in tow, as Naaman anticipated their encounter.

But it didn't go the way Naaman expected. God had another plan.

Now, Naaman was right to go for it.
He was right to step out in faith and pursue an encounter with the Lord *via the prophet Elisha*.
Naaman was right to bring gifts for Elisha.
Here was a man who understood showing honor.
As did the Shunamite woman, who also gained her blessing by showing honor.

Yes, as a man who had served in the military, Naaman understood rank and file.
He understood the power of displaying one's honor to a superior. In this case, Elisha was a superior in the spirit.
Yes, Naaman was a man who, having served royalty, knew the importance of approaching with an opulent offering.

Everything seemed on track for Naaman to walk right into a miracle, but again, things didn't go the way Naaman expected them to… not at first.

Elisha wouldn't see him.
There was no knocking on Elisha's door, having the prophet emerge with great pomp and circumstance to do a jaw dropping miracle - which is probably what Naaman expected and hoped for.

Instead, the prophet sent his assistant, with a message. That message contained a detailed instruction for Naaman. If Naaman would follow a simple instruction, to wash himself seven times in the river Jordan, healing could be his.

Immediately offended and disenfranchised, Naaman would have none of it. He rattled off rivers that he thought were superior to all the waters of Israel, and turned to leave in a rage.

It was Naaman's own servants who intervened. They convinced Naaman to (*listen carefully*) step out of pride, put aside his feelings, and at least try… instead of judging the instruction of the prophet. They pointed out how amazing and totally awe-inspiring it would be if it turned out God really did heal Naaman… by just seven dips in an Israeli river.

PROPHETIC NOTE TO YOU: **Please don't scoff at a prophetic instruction. Please don't ever dishonor the prophet because the word**

or the method are not what you expected or prefer. God's true prophets only repeat what they hear *Him* say, understanding that God's ways are not our ways. The Lord's ways are higher and often involve spiritual, elemental, supernatural or faith-linked things that we cannot comprehend.

How many of God's people miss a miracle because they dishonor or dismiss the prophet? How many blessings and breakthroughs are never received because someone scoffs at the word or dishonors the vessel? The principles in this timeless, powerful account of Naaman and Elisha, speak through the millennia, to educate and properly position you today.

Don't miss your miracle because you're ticked off for any reason! Let us stay humble in heart - miracles hang in the balance!

How did Naaman's situation turn out? Well, in the end, with nothing to lose and everything to gain, Naaman decided to follow Elisha's unconventional prophetic instruction, and he was not disappointed!

I'm sure he felt a little foolish, dunking himself precisely seven times in a river, in front of his servants, no less! The same servants who used to be in awe of his position but now knew of his debilitating disease. But faith rose up in Naaman that day; he had hope to receiving the fullness of the prophetic word. The Bible records the outcome:

2 Kings 5:14
So he went down and dipped himself in the Jordan seven times, as the man of God had told him, and his flesh was restored and became clean like that of a young boy. (NIV)

Let's go deeper. For the Lord desires your faith to be on fire, kindled to believe for mind-blowing miracles! Glory to God!

A situation very similar to that of Naaman, occurs just one chapter earlier in the Bible. Here we find a certain widow whose husband had left her in debt when he died. Elisha is used by God to work another incredible miracle for her, as recorded in *2 Kings 4:1-7*.

The Word records that her husband was a son of the prophets, considered a servant of Elisha, and that in life, he feared the Lord. I believe these details are included in the Bible on purpose. For they are very telling and they provide a powerful lesson for us. From these details we learn that sadly, it is possible to be closely associated with a true prophet, even a prophet who is anointed for the release of finance, and still somehow miss it.

How this man sat under Elisha's anointing and never learned how to access resources and prosperity, I don't know. I have questions. Did this man honor Elisha? We know that another of Elisha's servants mentioned, Gehazi, had a problem with faith, vision, loyalty, integrity and greed. Was this widow's late husband the same way? Had he too walked in dishonor toward the prophet of God? Why hadn't he ever learned the principles Elijah had passed on to Elisha, the principles Elisha consistently displayed in his ministry?

Here again, uncommon details within an urgent scenario. Here again, strong yet necessary lessons and Biblical teaching.

Once again, deep wisdom for the ones who will glean it. Yet once again deep revelation on the connection between faith, honor, obedience, and attaining the miracles of God.

When the Lord first showed me these revelatory teachings, the gravity shook me to my core and I listened intently; I learned. Are you listening now? Are you learning? Will you be one of the uncommon ones who walks in uncommon faith, honor and obedience… so as to attain and receive truly uncommon miracles by the power of the Lord?

Those miracles will sometimes come through an anointed prophet! Those miracles will sometimes come with a prophetic word coupled with a prophetic instruction! Will you be one who dares to believe, receive, and do? For I decree and declare in the mighty name of Jesus, this is your miracle season - and some of your most prolific miracles will be in the realm of supernatural healing, uncommon health and multiplication of your money supply! Somebody receive that by faith, and why don't you *SHOUT!* in Jesus' name?!

Precious child of God, it is heartbreaking yet true, some people can have full access to a vessel who's been anointed by the Lord to flow in miracles, but those people will never access those miracles. As with the example of Jesus in *Matthew 13:58*, where He could only do a few miracles because of the peoples' disbelief, the ones who don't receive a miracle will have that experience because of their own deficit somewhere, not because God missed it. God doesn't miss it. Sadly, many people do.

I pray with all my heart, that will never be you. Let God minister to you, in this. Please don't miss the weight of this revelation. I believe God is talking to someone today, about honor, integrity and correct posture toward appointed leaders… and how the presence of those things can lead to promotion and destiny (as with Elijah and Elisha) but their absence can lead to financial struggle, even premature or untimely death.

There in *2 Kings 4*, Elisha doesn't bother with the details; the woman is in real crisis, after all.

The creditors were coming to take her sons into legal slavery, a common judicial action of the day, toward debtors.

Elisha asks her a question: What shall I do for you? Tell me, what do you have in the house?

The woman says she has nothing but a jar of oil.

That's enough for the man of God! I can almost hear Elisha saying, "I can work with that!"

Oh, we serve a God of creation and multiplication!
We serve the God who makes a way where there is no way!
We serve the God who goes into every detail and causes us to prevail!
We serve a supernatural, commodity increasing, endless supply, No Limits God!

Elisha gives the widow woman a four-part instruction. Each aspect was crucial. Each instruction required full obedience. First, she was to go to her neighbors and borrow as many jars and vessels as she could. Second, she was to make sure to gather a multitude, not just a few. Third, that widow woman was instructed to return to her home, go inside with just her sons, and close the door. Then, she was to start pouring.

If I was there, I would surely have been shouting: *Pour, woman, pour!*

And when the oil stayed, ceasing to pour because she'd filled her last vessel, I'd have likely swatted those boys upside their heads and screamed, *I told you to help your mother find as many vessels as possible? Next time get more, ya got it?!*

Yes, because what do you think would have happened if that widow woman had more jars that day? You're right, the oil would have kept on flowing. What stopped the oil? The lack of a vessel to pour it into.

Why was it important for the woman to close the door? Because not everyone should see your miracle. Not everyone should have access to the power of God as it works in your life; what's for you is for you. Yes, and not everyone believes as you believe; if disbelief blocked the power of God from flowing abundantly in *Matthew 13*, then we must learn to shield our atmosphere from the poison of disbelief; doing so creates an environment that is conducive to miracles and welcoming to the power of God.

Why were the woman's sons to be present? Well, do you think those boys wanted Elisha's prophetic instruction to work? Do you think they were desperate for a miracle? You bet they were, so you can also be sure their faith was high. Here, we learn the importance of shutting out contamination by faithless people, and the cumulative power of faith-filled people. If one can put a thousand to flight, two can put ten thousand to flight. Three people, all of whom loved God, desperately wanting to see a miracle, faith-filled and believing for God's power to show up, pulled from the spirit, successfully! See this. Learn from this.

And now let's learn from this, too: it all began with a prophetic instruction.

Naaman was given a prophetic instruction.
The widow woman was given a prophetic instruction.
Their obedience mixed with faith, brought forth the miracle.

It was the way they honored the prophet and his words, that put them in position to receive.

The miracle was always there, ready to burst onto the scene! But it was their faith and obedience, together with their respect and honor for God's prophet, that allowed the miracle to birth into the natural.

Remember this chapter, meditate on these anointed words. For in just a few pages, I will give you a prophetic instruction!

As in the days of old, some of you will soon see a miracle of Biblical proportions in your life! You will be blessed, and God will be glorified. Hallelujah!

DR. JOLYNNE WHITTAKER

Chapter Ten

Your Holiness Is A Weapon: Maintain and Wield It! Your Righteousness Is A Garment: Keep It On!

DR. JOLYNNE WHITTAKER

This entire chapter is a strong prophetic word. This entire chapter is also a very, very necessary warning.

If the devil does not want God's people to prosper lest they become confident and empowered, please believe the devil really doesn't want any of God's people to be wealthy.

Now, of course that is too bad, because here you are and you are well on your way!
You are rising into an anointed position in the body of Christ, with many financial milestones and elevations to come! In Jesus' name.

The Bible reveals common tactics the devil uses in attempts to bring God's people down.
Heed these prophetic warnings well. Below I am exposing a few, that you may be aware and equipped to walk in mega victory.

Beware the attempt to lure you outside of reliance upon the Lord.
We see this demonstrated in the relentless attacks upon Jesus Himself, in *Luke 4:1-13*. Once it was substantiated that Jesus was in fact the prophesied Messiah, come to be the Deliverer and King of God's people, the onslaught began. The devil showed up and again and again, Satan attempted to get Jesus to do or say something that would defy God's directives and protocols.

Christ would have been completely justified to defend Himself, argue (and establish) various points, demonstrate His divinity and shut the entire exchange down. The legal accusation from Satan would have been pride, without a doubt. Instead, Jesus quoted Scripture in every instance Satan tried to bait Him. Eventually and inevitably Satan gave up and walked away.

Here comes your word: Once the devil substantiates the anointing you carry and your identity in the spirit, a test is sure to come. Stand. And having done all, stand! Do not get in your flesh and don't allow yourself to be baited. See the attack for what it is: a blatant attempt to interrupt and cancel your destiny. But as Jesus showed us, if you don't give up, the devil will. Cling to Scripture. Quote it out loud. Thinking Bible verses will not be enough; you'll need to speak God's Word aloud into the atmosphere. Remember, everything must respond to the Word of God. As you quote the Bible in moments of trial and test, you will see the test pass and you will access a new level every time. When the test ended for Jesus, He immediately launched into His ministry. Catch it! Temptation comes before Elevation!

The attempt to lure you into sin.
The Word says Be ye holy, for I am holy. What fellowship does darkness have with light? Nothing. What business does an anointed servant of the Lord have, cohosting with godless people and sitting with sinners? Absolutely none.

Mind you, we love people. We seek to bless people. We seek to minister and love them out of death, to life. Jesus went to the sinners, and many of us will too. But coming in the name of the Lord to be a blessing or deliver a message of hope, is starkly different than hanging out and hanging with, the self-chosen ungodly.

I always told my children; you can't stand in the mud puddle without getting mud on you. Now I tell the same thing to believers and spiritual sons and daughters. It is an accurate analogy and a true statement. Often, the devil begins the attempt to lure you into sin, by getting you connected to the wrong people, arranging for you to be in the wrong place, putting unholy things in front of your eyes, hoping you'll be seduced.

Don't fall for it. Your holiness is a weapon, and the devil knows it. Your purity is protection, satan knows that too. Your righteousness is a garment that keeps you within the provisional sphere of God's blessing. See the sinister agenda of luring you into sin. It is always for the purpose of stealing, killing and destroying — always. It may not start out that intense, but that is where it is going, mark my words.

The Bible says the wages of sin are death, plain and simple. You may think you have the strength, discipline, self-control or fortitude to reel yourself in before something gets too bad. You may believe that you'll be able to vacate the premises before something unholy happens. Wrong! Sin starts subtle, and it is seductive. The devil is simply slow-rolling you to an expected end: steal, kill, destroy — that's it, always.

If Sampson could sit you down and tell you the truth, he'd tell you he regrets ever getting involved with Delilah. Yes, the Lord restored Sampson's strength and used him to gain a massive victory, but at what cost? Sampson lost his dignity, his anointing, his destined future, his eyes — my God, what else did he lose in that process? And none of it had to happen. The devil made sure to dangle the poison of Sampson's choice in front of him, too; the scriptures reveal Sampson always had a weakness for Philistine women, that's why his parents tried to drive it home that Sampson was called to marry a good woman of the Lord.

Was Delilah a woman of the Lord? No, she was a Philistine, forbidden fruit. Sampson's downfall began with disobedience, and that disobedience occurred because Sampson decided to partake of the sinful thing he enjoyed. Stay so far away from sin, for so long, that it never, ever, seems enjoyable to you. Sampson's humiliation, torture, anguish, agony, and untimely death… were not enjoyable. Let us learn.

David was a man after God's own heart, and he remains a strong example to us in so many ways. The Psalms are priceless, absolutely priceless. But if David could sit down with you over a cup of coffee, he might admit a few things he dearly regrets. How many sleepless nights did David have, over deliberately arranging the murder of Uriah? How often did David regret ever letting his gaze linger upon the naked and bathing Bathsheba? Yes, David married her but that did not erase the stench or stain of their sin; the child they bore in their unholy union, died as a baby, unleashing grief we can only imagine. It didn't have to happen.

Don't go where you're not supposed to go. Don't linger who you're not supposed to linger with. Don't look at things that wouldn't make God proud of you, and don't look for ways you can straddle the fence and try to live in both worlds. You are in this world but not of this world; should you try to live with one foot in Heaven and the other in satan's playground, then it's only a matter of time before your anointing is stripped, as well. I can't water down these words and I can't soften it around the edges. It is what it is. Sin will kill you. Don't give the devil a chance to prove he is a murderer. Sin will block you. You've not come this far to live a mediocre or unblessed life. God has another road for you. He is calling you higher. Selah.

Scriptural References: 1 Peter 1:16, Romans 6:23, John 10:10, Psalm 1:1-3, Judges 16, 2 Samuel 12

The blatant attempt to get you to switch sides.

The audacity of the devil to actually try to make a deal with Jesus! Did you catch that in *Matthew 4:9*? Yes, because the devil knows wealth and power are very powerful temptations. How many people come to mind when you think of corrupt individuals who have power and wealth? Many. Way too many.

Wealth comes from one of two places: from the devil or from God. That's it. In this current world system, big money comes by The Blessing and Anointing of the Lord, or it comes from the temporary ruler of this world.

In *Mark 4:9*, the enemy offers wealth and power, indeed all the kingdoms of this world to Jesus, because until King Jesus establishes the Kingdom here on earth, those things are Satan's to give.

That explains why so many celebrities in the entertainment industries, such as film and music, fall into satanic habits and lifestyles. Some make a literal pact with the devil. That also explains why some of the wealthiest industries and arenas, like the fashion industry and politics, are rife with human trafficking, unholy satanic rituals, drug addiction and alcoholism, and so much more. Many who get involved in these industries lose their minds or lose their lives, and this is why.

Well, why in the world did they get involved in the first place?? Many were naive and didn't know any better. Some, however, did know, and they were willing to pay the price. Some get in and can't get out. Others get in and don't want to get out; they switch over to the dark and perverse side. They become lust-filled over the money and power they have, and they're hungry for more at any cost. I have seen some become completely demonized and depraved; I can always tell by their eyes and their mannerisms, no matter how good they think they are at hiding the demon they have inside of them.

I have known people who prosper in the Lord

and become completely intoxicated on their prosperity. This grieves my spirit, because I know the blessing cannot last. If a servant of God gone rogue won't self-correct and clean their house, God will do it for them. It's only a matter of time.

I have watched some very anointed preachers and worshipers gain a measure of fame and fall in love with the spotlight. They become puffed up with pride, completely ignorant to their own folly and ungodliness. These too won't last forever; God chastises those He loves, and that includes those who used to serve Him in purity. Never forget, it is the Lord your God who opens doors *and* closes doors. It is the Lord who raises one up, and sits another down. The mighty hand of God is in charge of promotions and demotions in the Kingdom, never forget it.

Yes, and a closing word to the wise before I move on from this paragraph: never think others are responsible to promote or position you. I know God will use some people to open doors, but they are not God nor do they have the final say in your destiny. Some people think they can control how high you go or if you elevate at all. Some believe if they don't support you, you'll never get anywhere at all. This wrong thinking causes them to believe they are in control of your opportunities and your destiny. Not so. God sits in the Heavens and laughs.

Rely not on man to promote you. Never kiss up or try to finagle a promotion. Stay faithful, stay holy, stay ready, and stay bowed low at Jesus' feet. In due season, God will put you on. Selah. That was a whole prophetic word for somebody!

Yet as for the ones who tried to block you or keep you low, they will see it when you are blessed. They will see it when the hand of the Lord promotes you. God will prepare a table for you in the presence of your enemies, and every slandering tongue thou shalt condemn. Receive that in Jesus' name! Yes, and do not think it strange when the very ones who sought to block you… are ringside to watch your elevation! — *Daniel 2:21, Psalm 75:6-7, Isaiah 22:22*

Child of God, do not fall into sin.
Do not return to old sin.
Do not come into alliance with the devil in an attempt to elevate.
Stay strong in the Lord.
Stay pure before the Lord.

Your holiness is a weapon! Your holiness will protect you!
Your righteousness is a blessing! Righteousness attracts the Lord's blessing!
Receive that in Jesus' name.

Let's go even deeper still…

DR. JOLYNNE WHITTAKER

Chapter Eleven

God Will Reveal Methods and Strategies... So You Can Access Wealth

DR. JOLYNNE WHITTAKER

Many of your wealth sources will come from the Lord in the form of idea or an instruction. The Lord may give you a vision or a directive.

If you, as His anointed vessel, will pursue and follow the path of ideas and instructions God gives you, you will find yourself in a flurry of growth and expansion.

You will begin to experience a God-given excitement that will become familiar over the years, as everything you need to know will be downloaded to you, resources and connections strategically appear, and doors open before you. Then, the harvest of the instruction will come. You will flow in the supernatural anointing of the assignment, and the result will be the cultivation of wealth.

This is something you will become used to. I have seen the Lord give ideas and instructions again and again, to myself and others. In time, you will come to easily recognize the voice of the Lord, and you will again return to the anointed space of Kingdom wealth creation.

The Bible reveals that God gives spiritual gifs to men (and women). Often, your spiritual gifting will be relevant, useful or required, in the cultivation or acquisition of wealth.

However, God gives practical gifts to men and women, too. Read this scripture:

Daniel 1:17
To these four young men God gave knowledge and understanding of all kinds of literature and learning. And Daniel could understand visions and dreams of all kinds. (NIV)

Much of your natural gifting is not natural at all, but supernaturally given to you by Almighty God. For the Lord will equip you for every good work you are called to. Glory to God!

Your gifting has a purpose.
Your gifting is strategic.
Your gifting is a divine insertion by the mighty hand of your Creator.
God has designed you for your destiny - get that in your spirit!

The Word also says God gave Daniel an excellent spirit. It was this excellence, which we can also refer to as work ethic or integrity, that distinguished Daniel from others, and set him apart for promotion. From this we see that God will instill strong character in some, and that too will be relevant and useful in their destiny. Glory to God! — Daniel 6:3

The Word of God teaches us that it is our unique gifting that makes room for us, even bringing us before great men. Expect your natural gifting to be a strong tool when it comes to connections and opportunities. These too are connected to the cultivation and acquisition of wealth. — Proverb 18:16

There will be times when you receive a unique wisdom, and that wisdom, when applied, will usher wealth into your life.

There will be times when God quite literally gives you a witty invention, something unique and creative. This may be an invention that can be produced and sold, or it can be an idea to apply to your business, ministry or finances. The result will always be twofold: you will be on the cutting edge, and you will acquire wealth.

Always take God's wisdom and witty inventions very, very seriously.
Never dismiss them.

Never, ever, allow your mental mind to interfere with a supernatural download from the Lord. Never let your own thoughts convince you the idea is impractical or unlikely. When God gives you divine wisdom or a witty idea, it doesn't have to be practical or "doable" in your mind; God is not summoning you to a round-table discussion where you will chime in with what you think of the idea or instruction. No, God will always tell you a sure thing. He'll give you a sure thing! The invention will be sure to prosper, should you pursue and do it! The wisdom will be sure to perform and bring forth great prosperity, should you trust and apply it!

Read and receive:

> *Proverb 8:12*
> *I, wisdom, dwell with prudence; and find out knowledge of witty inventions.*
> *(KJV)*

> *Isaiah 45:3*
> *And I will give thee the treasures off darkness, and hidden riches of secret places, that thou mayest know that I, the Lord, which call thee by thy name, am the God of Israel. (KJV)*

> *Deuteronomy 8:18*
> *But remember the LORD your God, for it is he who gives you the ability to produce wealth, and so confirms his covenant, which he swore to your ancestors, as it is today.*
> *(NIV)*

To whom much is given, much is required.
This is not an anointing for the lazy or complacent.

In order to receive a portion of the coming wealth transfer, the only requirements that must meet, are for you to be holy, obedient, and a good steward.

However, wealth ideas and instructions are not given to the lazy hand or the slack hand.

Read and receive:

> *Proverb 10:4*
> *Lazy hands make for poverty, but diligent hands bring wealth. (NIV)*

Selah. Oh, glory to God and selah again!

Let the redeemed of the Lord say so, and let the diligent hand receive a generous portion! In the name of Jesus!

This short but powerful chapter is your compass, your confirmation, and your personal prophetic word. Do all things as unto the Lord, and do so heartily and with excellence. Maintain a diligent hand and a hunger for divine wisdom, and wealth and riches will ever be in your home!

Your family will never be under a generational curse; as for you and your house, you will serve the Lord and you will flow in GENERATIONAL BLESSINGS!

This too is how all nations of the world will come to know you are called by the name of the Lord, and fear you. For no system or agenda of man will ever be able to impoverish or bankrupt you, for you have been anointed and appointed for Kingdom Wealth! In the mighty name of Jesus Christ our King!

Psalm 112:1-3
Praise the LORD. Blessed are those who fear the LORD, who find great delight in his commands. Their children will be mighty in the land; the generation of the upright will be blessed. Wealth and riches are in their houses, and their righteousness endures forever. (NIV)

Deuteronomy 28:10
Then all the peoples on earth will see that you are called by the name of the LORD, and they will fear you. (NIV)

Chapter Twelve

Urgent Prophetic Words for You… *Right Now!*

DR. JOLYNNE WHITTAKER

Dear Reader:

If the Lord sent me to your home to deliver Prophetic Insights and Wisdom to you, regarding this path of Kingdom Millionaire you have been called to walk... here is what I would tell you, readily and very seriously. It is my hope you regard and receive these words with the utmost of attentiveness and urgency. These are things every Kingdom Millionaire must hear and know, and they are my parting prophetic gift, to you.

— Dr. JoLynne Whittaker

Please know this... Family will respond to your increased financial status in interesting and sometimes unexpected ways. Some will go quiet, others will take on an air of disdain, while others are emboldened to approach you for financial loans again and again. Only the ones who ask questions are genuinely interested in how you did it. Only the ones who are not the least bit jealous, will ask you any questions or make any comment at all. Many will be oddly and very tellingly, quiet.

Now of course, you didn't do it, the Lord did it for you. Your wealth has come from the Lord; even so, do not be surprised when many do not want to talk to you about your increased financial status. They sense the conversation will eventually lead to Jesus, and they don't want to be led to Jesus. They *do* want access to your blessing, but they *don't* want to know the Blesser. They *do* want to sit (and dine) at your table, but they *don't* want to know the One who built and laid the table.

Yes, it will be heartbreaking in many cases. And yet, from talking to others who have walked this path before me and before you, I have learned this always seems to be the way. Jesus told us many would reject Him. It is that simple… and that profound.

Give to others according to the instruction and leading of the Lord. There will be times the Lord tells you to bless or help a family member or friend. I am not talking about sowing or tithing, I am talking about blessing others with money.

See any money you give them, as a gift. Even if

they assure you it's only a loan, I strongly urge you to see it as a gift, because only rarely will the money ever come back to you. Most will not repay, and over time when they do not or cannot pay you back, that will lead to awkwardness or embarrassment on their part.

So do not be surprised if some of the people you bless, eventually distance themselves. They will cease talking to you, cease reaching out to you, cease responding to you - even though good manners and honor would dictate differently, because *you're* the one who blessed *them*.

What a strange dichotomy, right? You helped them, but they go silent on you, eventually go missing.

It will help to remind yourself they're probably feeling embarrassed. Or perhaps they were never as morally sound as you thought they were.

See that money you gave them as a gift, like so many gifts the Lord has given you. Your generosity meets the criteria of *Luke 6:38*, which means the Lord Himself will repay you. Rest in that. And rest knowing you have shown your God that you are a giver. He will reward you with more seed. — *2 Corinthians 9:10*

Never let yourself be taken advantage of serially. This must be said, because like a moth to a flame, many will come, thinking you are now their ATM. It pains me to say but nevertheless it is true: many have become professional takers. That is, they are very comfortable asking others for money. They would rather have someone temporarily help them out of the trouble they're in, than make the changes required to permanently get out of the trouble they're in.

Perhaps they don't realize they can get out. Some people become convinced, often after years of hardship, that financial struggle is simply the way life is, for them. They don't know sound Biblical principles regarding God's Covenant with His people, Salvation, Access and Restoration by the Blood Covenant of Jesus Christ. Nor do they understand Dominion and Financial Blessing by the Abrahamic Covenant. They may love Jesus with their whole heart, but they do not have a real understanding or revelation of true and holy Biblical prosperity.

I was shocked by the ministers who began approaching me for money, and very comfortably so. Here I was relatively new to ministry, while many of them were lifelong ministers! A few of them were lifelong takers, as well. I noticed they very comfortable approaching others for money. They quote *Matthew 7:7*, as though that verse means we are to ask other people for money. The day they get a revelation that *Matthew 7:7* means ask the Father, their life will begin to change. Please be wise. Be wise as a serpent yet harmless as a dove; don't be naive yet don't let your heart become hardened. The professional takers are out there and they've got a nose for money.

Help when God tells you to. Give when He tells you to. But understand you are also responsible for protecting and multiplying the resources God gives you. Don't allow what God put you in charge of, to be drained.

Never disconnect from the Vine. Stay close to Jesus and bowed low at His feet, at all costs! He is the Vine, you are the branch. Stay connected! Stay alive!

It is only a matter of time before the world tries to woo you into seeing wealth as they do, which is a satanic agenda to get you to cross over into materialism. Don't do it. Your life is not your own, you were bought with a price. Many have walked this path, crashed and burned, and they are no more. You are not irreplaceable. However, God does love and want you. So, stay connected to the Vine! This part is on you.

I have watched some ministers become very smitten with the prosperity God gave them. So much so, they become more about the trappings of financial success than they do the Kingdom of Jesus Christ. There is no question, wealth can be seductive. In order to maintain a correct posture and perspective, you simply *must* stay at the feet of Jesus! In that position, you will never lose sight of his whip-scarred back or his nail-scarred hands and feet. Staying close to your King will maintain your footing in reality.

Do not be hesitant or embarrassed to be Royal. Here is a truth: the Lord will give you the finest life has to offer, for He desires you to live as a King or Queen, even His Priest, in the earth. We see this principle in place when Joseph went to Potiphar's house, it was very appropriate that Joseph look like an Egyptian in order to operate within the locale and environment of his assignment. That same principle displayed itself when Ruth went to that life-changing meeting with Boaz. Naomi made it clear to Ruth that it was prudent that she dresses for where she was going. — *Genesis 41:37-44, Ruth 3:1-3*

Realms and rooms have codes of conduct and also codes of attire. God's Kingdom Millionaires know this. We understand it very well. We don't dress down to fit the room. We dress royal and the room rises to meet us.

The prideful or rebellious may buck against it, but wealthy Kingdom Ambassadors have the wisdom to understand dressing for the mantle *and* the assignment. We are representing the King; of course we present and conduct ourselves as royal in the earth.

We will always be humble enough to adjust ourselves accordingly, allowing the Lord to upgrade, tweak, prune and present us as a living example of His abundance and royalty. But we do not fall in love with what He gives us. In reality, it's nothing in comparison to what is coming in Heaven! We do not become awestruck by the trappings of a prosperous life; they're just things after all. Our destination is a restored Kingdom on earth that can never be shaken, one where we will live in glorified bodies, forever with our precious and beloved King, Christ Jesus!

Oh, that is as real to me as this coffee I'm sipping right now! It is as real to me as the sound of these computer keys beneath my fingertips! Let it be as real, to you.

Remember these words, always.
I'm prophesying to you right now!
Take good care of what God gives you, but never fall in love with money or the things it can buy.

Stay strong in Jesus. Stay bowed low, ever at His feet. He is the Vine… you are the branch.

If you want to stay alive, if you want to keep growing, if you want to be healthy and strong, vibrant and never wither, *STAY CONNECTED TO THE VINE!* The moment you start to wander from Christ Jesus… a sure withering has begun. Remember this well! —*John 15:5*

The Lord will expect you to be a good steward of what He gives you. Be it a business, a ministry, an assignment, a home, a marriage, a car, a vision, a family, a staff, a property, etc. Notice I've deliberately named several different things. That's because every good gift and every perfect gift comes down from the Father of lights, in Whom is no variableness, neither shadow of turning.

This means that God does not change, like the seasons do. God does not change, like people do. Your Heavenly Father is the giver of good gifts and He is the giver of perfect gifts (two categories!) and He desires to see us appreciate, steward, and care for what He gives us.

All throughout the Bible, God speaks to us about the quality of our work. We are taught the importance of having an excellent spirit and being trustworthy as a steward. God desires us to be sober and integral. Never stray from the Lord's standard of excellence, faithfulness, and purity. I repeat once again: never fall in love with things God gives you. Don't allow yourself to become comfortable with the life God elevates you into, for this leads to becoming casual because without realizing it, you've begun taking God's goodness, grace and generosity, for granted.

Never let it be so.
Some do, but not you.
Some will, but you won't.

Always keep your eyes on the prize, on the high calling in Christ Jesus, and God will take you from glory to glory! Hallelujah!

— James 1:17, 1 Peter 4:10, 1 Corinthians 4:2, Colossians 3:23, Philippians 3:14

The reading of this book marks a new beginning for you. You are accessing a new level, and it will change your life and your future, in Jesus' name.

King Jesus is returning soon for a glorious Church without spot, blemish or wrinkle. He is returning in hopes of finding faith-filled Christians who are occupying until His arrival. That will be YOU!

These principles are going to ignite a deeper study of the Scriptures in your life, and greater hunger for the Lord!

As new things arrive, you will find the prophetic advice and insight required, to win every battle and elevate continually. May the Lord cover your life and bless you abundantly! May you shine and do exploits for the glory of the King!

As the wealth of the wicked is released into the Body of Christ, may a generous portion fall into your hands. May you always hear the voice of God and go where you're supposed to go! Sow where you're supposed to sow! Leap when God tells you to leap! Wait when He tells you to wait, and move on the wisdom and instructions He gives you to access new dimensions - in Jesus' name!

I bless you in the name of the Lord.
Godspeed and God bless you abundantly,
Kingdom Millionaire!

Dr. JoLynne Whittaker was born in Rochester, New York to a single-mother household. She grew up in the inner city, was raised Catholic, and knew from childhood that she would serve the Lord with her life.

From a very young age, Dr. Whittaker's prophetic anointing displayed itself. From its early days, her ministry unto the Lord has grown and thrived under the leading of the Holy Ghost.

She is the author of five books, including this one. Her other titles are listed on the following page.

Dr. Whittaker can be seen preaching and prophesying the word of the Lord on National Television three times each week on three separate national networks. Her ministry also livestreams two additional broadcasts each week.

You can learn more about the ministry of Dr. JoLynne Whittaker, including her Television and online service schedule, on her website. There you can also order her books and partner with the dynamic prophetic ministry Jesus has called her into.

Dr. Whittaker travels between two ministry headquarters and full-scale television studios in both Western New York and South Florida in the Gulf of Mexico. She receives prayer requests and prayers for friends of the ministry, daily.

STEPPING INTO FAVOR - In this book you will learn what the Bible teaches about the favor of God and how to access it! The Lord wants to open doors for you, bless you, protect and prosper you. Perhaps your life doesn't feel favored and blessed right now but it's time to change that! It's your time to step into God's favor!

IT'S TIME TO SOAR - There is a reason some people elevate and others don't. There is also a way to accelerate personal elevation into the will of God for your life! The delay is over, acceleration and elevation are here! In this best-selling book, Dr. JoLynne Whittaker breaks down essential Biblical principals required for your shift. Get ready, this is your season!

DATE WITH DESTINY - In Spring of 2011, the Lord led Dr. JoLynne Whittaker to a run-down lakehouse on the secluded shores of Lake Ontario. There, God taught her the secret to finding your purpose, and that second chances and true love are possible, when we let Jesus lead the way! This special book is filled with scripture, prophetic words, and raw transparency about Dr. JoLynne's story. Reading this book will be your date with destiny because a brand new season is coming for you!

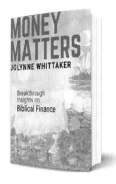

MONEY MATTERS - God desires you to be a good steward of your money so you can live as the head, and not the tail. In this practical handbook, Dr. Whittaker will teach you sound Biblical doctrine that will help you to increase financially. God has instruction for increase in your money matters! *Free Download on Our Website.

This is our book on Salvation by Christ Jesus, and it answers all the tough questions. Such as: If there is a God, why is there evil in the world? If God loves me, why is my life so hard? Free copies of this book are sent to jails, prisons, and substance abuse rehab centers. Request one for your loved one or order, on our website.

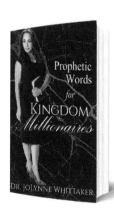

PROPHETIC WORDS for KINGDOM MILLIONAIRES - God is raising up millionaires for such a time as this! These are passionate followers of King Jesus who have accessed the Blessing of the Lord and become highly favored and prosperous financially. Are you destined to be a Kingdom Millionaire? If so, this book is for you! The Biblical principles and prophetic words in this book are solid gold! You will go to this book again and again, as you increase in the prosperity of the Lord and occupy the millionaire anointing!